Labour Law in Croatia

Labour Law in Croatia

Third Edition

Ivana Grgurev

This book was originally published as a monograph in the International Encyclopaedia of Laws/Labour Law and Industrial Relations.

Founding Editor: Roger Blanpain
General Editor: Frank Hendrickx
Volume Editor: Roger Blanpain

Wolters Kluwer

Published by:
Kluwer Law International B.V.
PO Box 316
2400 AH Alphen aan den Rijn
The Netherlands
E-mail: lrs-sales@wolterskluwer.com
Website: www.wolterskluwer.com/en/solutions/kluwerlawinternational

Sold and distributed by:
Wolters Kluwer Legal & Regulatory U.S.
920 Links Avenue
Landisville, PA 17538
United States of America
E-mail: customer.service@wolterskluwer.com

ISBN 978-94-035-2789-5

e-Book: ISBN 978-94-035-2829-8
web-PDF: ISBN 978-94-035-2839-7

This title is available on www.kluwerlawonline.com

The Author

Professor Ivana Grgurev graduated in Law in 1997 from the Faculty of Law, University of Zagreb. She has held an Doctor of Juridical Science (SJD) at the Faculty of Law, University of Zagreb, since 2006. She is a tenured full professor at the Chair of Labour Law and Social Security Law, University of Zagreb. She was a member of working groups for drafting several pieces of national legislation (such as the Anti-discrimination Act and the Maternity and Parental Benefits Act). Professor Grgurev was a member of the Working Group for the Preparation of Negotiation on the Accession of the Republic of Croatia to the European Union (Negotiation Chapter 19: Employment and Social Policy). She is a national expert in the European Labour Law Network and a researcher in the project 'Restatement of the Labour Law in Europe'. She is a member of the National Council for Social Policy, as well as a member of the working group for the development of the National Plan for Suppression of Sexual Violence and Sexual Harassment for the period from 2022 to 2027. She was a visiting professor at the Law Faculty of the University of Trento (Italy) and University College Dublin (UCD) (Ireland). In the academic years 2015/2016 and 2016/2017, she was vice dean at the Faculty of Law, University of Zagreb. She has published several books and many articles in the field of labour law (anti-discrimination law, collective agreements, managerial contracts, etc.).

The Author

Table of Contents

The Author 3

List of Abbreviations 11

General Introduction 13

Chapter 1. The General Background 13

§1. GEOGRAPHY 13

§2. POPULATION 13

§3. POLITICAL SYSTEM 13

§4. POPULATION AND EMPLOYMENT STATISTICS 16

Chapter 2. Definitions and Notions 20

§1. LABOUR LAW 20
I. Individual Labour Law 20
II. Collective Labour Law 20

§2. SOCIAL SECURITY LAW 21

Chapter 3. The Role of Government 22

§1. THE AUTONOMY OF SOCIAL PARTNERS 22

§2. GOVERNMENT INSTITUTIONS 22

Chapter 4. Sources of Labour Law 23

§1. INTERNATIONAL AND EUROPEAN SOURCES 23
I. The International Labour Organizations 23
II. The Council of Europe 24

§2. NATIONAL SOURCES 24

I. Constitution 24
II. Ordinary Legislation 25
III. Court Decisions 26
IV. Collective Agreements 26
V. Works Agreements 28
VI. Employment Regulations 28
VII. Employment Contracts 28

§3. THE HIERARCHY OF THE SOURCES OF LABOUR LAW 29

Part I. Individual Employment Relationship 31

Chapter 1. Definitions and Concepts 31

§1. THE DEFINITION OF EMPLOYEE 31

§2. KINDS OF EMPLOYMENT CONTRACT 32
I. Contract for an Indefinite Period 32
II. Fixed-Term Contract 33
III. Part-Time Work 33
IV. Temporary Work 34

§3. SPECIAL GROUPS OF EMPLOYED PERSONS 35
I. Apprentices 35
II. Juveniles 36
III. Disabled Persons 36
IV. Foreign Employees 38
V. Posted Employees 40
VI. Pregnant Employees/Parents 41

Chapter 2. Duties of the Parties in the Course of the Employment Relationship 43

§1. DUTIES OF THE EMPLOYEE 43
I. Duty to Work 43
II. Ancillary Duties 43

§2. DUTIES OF THE EMPLOYER 44
I. Duty to Pay Remuneration 44
II. Duty to Employ the Employee 46
III. Duty of Equal Treatment 47

Chapter 3. Working Time, Public Holidays and Annual Leave 50

§1. WORKING TIME 50

§2. Overtime 52

§3. Night Work and Shift Work 52

§4. Work on Sundays and Public Holidays 53

§5. Annual Leave 54

§6. Breaks, Daily Rest, Paid and Unpaid Leave 55

§7. Maternity: Parental Leave – Breastfeeding Breaks 56

Chapter 4. Remuneration 59

§1. The Notion of Remuneration 59

§2. The Regulation of Remuneration 59

§3. Equal Pay 61

§4. Remuneration in Case of Temporary Non-performance of Work 62
I. Sickness 62
II. Pregnancy and Maternity 62

Chapter 5. Employee Liability 65

Chapter 6. Termination of Employment Contract 68

§1. The Death of the Employee or Employer; Termination of Small Business 68

§2. Expiry of the Fixed-Time Contract 68

§3. Retirement 69

§4. Termination by Mutual Consent 70

§5. General Work Incapacity 70

§6. Judicial Termination of the Contract 71

§7. Dismissal 71
I. Extraordinary Dismissal 71
II. Ordinary Dismissal 73

A. Just Causes 73
B. The Guarantee of a Minimum Term of Notice 75
III. Role of the Works Council in Dismissal Cases 76
IV. Special Protection for Specific Groups 78
A. Pregnancy and Parenthood 78
B. Disabled Employees 79
C. Apprentices 80
D. Members of Employee Representative Bodies 80
E. Shop Stewards 81
V. Collective Dismissals 81

Chapter 7. Non-competition Covenant, Employee Inventions 83

Chapter 8. Settlement of Individual Labour Disputes 86

Part II. Collective Labour Law 91

Chapter 1. Freedom of Association 91

Chapter 2. Trade Unions and the Employers' Associations 93

Chapter 3. Institutionalized Forms of Employee Participation 97

§1. Works Councils 97

§2. Employee Participation on the Employer's Boards (Supervisory Board, Board of Directors) 100

Chapter 4. Collective Bargaining 101

§1. Level and Scope of Collective Bargaining 101

§2. Parties to a Collective Agreement 102

§3. Content and Effect of a Collective Agreement 103
I. Obligatory Part 103
II. Normative Part 104

§4. Formal Requirements, Duration 105

§5. Extension of Collective Agreements by Governmental Decree 110

§6. Enforcement of the Collective Agreement 111

Chapter 5. Industrial Conflict 112

§1. STRIKES 112

§2. LOCK-OUTS 117

Selected Bibliography 119

Index 121

List of Abbreviations

CEFTA	Central European Free Trade Agreement
EEA	European Economic Area
EEIG	European Economic Interest Grouping
EU	European Union
ETUC	European Trade Union Confederation
GDP	Gross Domestic Product
HRK	Croatian Currency (*Hrvatska kuna*)
HZZO	Croatian Health Insurance Institute
IOE	International Organization of Employers
ILO	International Labour Organization
ITUC	International Trade Union Confederation
UN	United Nations
USD	United States Dollar
VSRH	Supreme Court of the Republic of Croatia

List of Abbreviations

General Introduction

Chapter 1. The General Background

§1. Geography

1. The Republic of Croatia (hereinafter 'Croatia') covers an area of 56,594 square kilometres. Croatia is situated in the south-eastern part of Europe. It borders Italy, Slovenia, Hungary, Serbia, Montenegro and Bosnia and Herzegovina. As it is situated on the Adriatic Sea, it is also considered a Mediterranean country.

§2. Population

2. Croatia has a population of about 3.87 million inhabitants with an average density of 68.1 inhabitants per square kilometre. Croatia has negative population growth. Women comprise 52% of the population, and men 48%. The average age of the population is 44.3 years (according to the 2022 data). Croats are the majority ethnic community (91.63% in 2021). Ethnic minorities make up the rest: Serbs (3.2%), Bosnians (0.62%), and a small number of Czechs, Albanians, Montenegrins, Hungarians, Macedonians, Germans and Austrians, Roma, Ruthenians, Slovaks, Slovenians, Italians and Ukrainians.

§3. Political System

3. Croatia is an independent, sovereign and democratic parliamentary republic, which won its independence on 8 October 1991 after being a part of the Socialist Federal Republic of Yugoslavia for decades. The Constitution of the Republic of Croatia entered into force on 22 December 1990. In the Amendments to the Constitution of the Republic of Croatia adopted in 2000, the semi-presidential system was replaced by a parliamentary system.

4. The preamble to the Constitution of the Republic of Croatia lists the documents which form the historical foundations and show the continued development of the state-building idea grounded in the historical right of the Croatian nation to full sovereignty, from the formation of the Croatian principalities in the seventh century until the decision of the Territorial Antifascist Council of the National Liberation of Croatia (1943), the Constitution of the People's Republic of Croatia (1947) and all the subsequent constitutions of the Socialist Republic of Croatia (1963–1990). Because of a shared legal heritage, it behoves us to mention that Croatia was part of the Austro-Hungarian Empire between 1867 and 1918. In 1918, it became part of the Kingdom of the Serbs, Croats and Slovenes (in 1929, the state was renamed the Kingdom of Yugoslavia). As a result of the Croatian nation's aspiration for greater autonomy, the Croatian *Banovina* was set up in 1939 as a territorial unit within the Kingdom of Yugoslavia. It existed until 1941. After the capitulation of Yugoslavia in 1941 until the end of World War II, the Yugoslav territory was occupied, and parts of it were annexed by the occupying states (Italy, Germany, Hungary and Bulgaria). In the parts of Croatia's territory not ruled directly by an occupying power, the Independent State of Croatia was established under the auspices of Nazi Germany and fascist Italy. At the same time, the Partisan authorities adopted various legal instruments in the parts they controlled. From 1945 to 1991, Croatia (and other states in existence today: Slovenia, Bosnia and Herzegovina, Serbia, Kosovo, Montenegro and Macedonia) was part of the Socialist Federal Republic of Yugoslavia (the state had three official names in its history; from 1963 on, it was called the Socialist Federal Republic of Yugoslavia).

5. The political system of Croatia is based on the principle of separation of powers into the legislative, executive and judicial branches, but there is also a constitutionally guaranteed right to local and regional self-government. The President of the Republic is the head of state, representing Croatia in the country and abroad. The President is elected directly by the citizens in a secret ballot based on universal suffrage. The President's term of office is five years. The President can stand for re-election once. The Croatian Parliament (*Sabor*) has legislative power. The members of the Croatian Parliament (whose number currently stands at 151) are elected by the citizens in a direct election for a term of office of four years. The Government of Croatia exercises executive power. It consists of a Prime Minister, one or more Deputy Prime Ministers and Ministers. In order for the Government to assume office, it must obtain the confidence of the majority of all the Members of Parliament. The Government is accountable to the Parliament. The Government of Croatia tables laws and other acts before the Croatian Parliament; proposes the central budget and annual accounts; executes laws and other decisions of the Croatian Parliament; adopts decrees to implement laws; conducts foreign and domestic policy; directs and controls the operation of the civil service; tends to the economic development of the country; and directs the performance and development of public services. Judiciary power is exercised by regular and specialized courts. The former are municipal and county courts and the Supreme Court of the Republic of Croatia (VSRH). The specialized courts are the misdemeanour courts, commercial courts, the High Misdemeanour Court of Croatia, and the Administrative Court of Croatia. There is a first instance Labour Court but solely in Zagreb. The VSRH is the highest court in Croatia. It is there to ensure a uniform application of the law and equality of citizens. The President of the Supreme Court is elected by the Parliament to a term of office of four years. The judges are appointed and dismissed in prescribed exceptional cases by the State Judicial Council. A term of judge's office is permanent. The State Judicial Council is a specialized body in the judiciary whose jurisdiction includes the appointment and dismissal of judges and adjudicating in disciplinary matters involving judges. It consists of eleven members: seven judges, two university law professors and two Members of Parliament, one of whom must be from an opposition party. The members of the State Judicial Council are elected to a term of office of four years and may be re-elected only once. The Constitutional Court of Croatia consists of thirteen judges elected by the Croatian Parliament to a term of office of eight years. Judges of the Constitutional Court must not perform any other public or professional duty. The Constitutional Court rules on the constitutionality of laws and on the constitutionality and legality of other regulations. The Constitutional Court can repeal laws or some of their provisions if it finds that they are not in accordance with the Constitution and other regulations or some of their provisions if it finds that they are not in accordance with the Constitution and the law. The Constitutional Court may annul a regulation or its provisions, taking into account all the circumstances important for the protection of constitutionality and legality, and especially the seriousness of the violation of the Constitution or the law, and the interest of legal certainty: if it violates the human rights and fundamental freedoms guaranteed by the Constitution and if it places some individuals, groups or associations in a more or a less privileged position unjustifiably.

6. The Croatian language and the Latin alphabet are official. The national currency is euro. Prior to 1 January 2023, the Croatian Currency was – *Hrvatska kuna* (HRK). The capital city is Zagreb. It has 767,131 inhabitants (2021). Municipalities and towns/cities are units of local self-government. Their main tasks pertain to providing for the citizens' needs in the sphere of spatial and urban planning, housing, municipal services, social assistance, primary healthcare, child care, primary education, culture, etc. All local and regional self-government units have their administrations and representative bodies (assemblies). Municipalities, as units of local self-government, usually cover several inhabited areas that form a natural, economic and social whole whose inhabitants share the same interests. Towns/cities are units of local self-government that either serve as county capitals or have more than 10,000 inhabitants and form an urban, historical, natural, economic and social whole. Exceptionally, if special circumstances (history, economy, geography and transport) call for it, other settlements that do not meet the general criteria can be established as towns/cities. Counties are units of regional self-government whose territory forms a whole based on its geographic features, traffic routes, history, economy, social features and self-government needs. It is established in order to take care of issues of regional concern. According to the Statistical Report published by the Croatian Bureau of Statistics, in 2021, there were 428 municipalities and 127 towns. Croatia is administratively divided into twenty counties and the City of Zagreb, which has a special status.

Croatia is a member of many supranational organizations such as the Council of Europe, the United Nations (UN), the International Labour Organization (ILO), the World Trade Organization, Central European Free Trade Agreement (CEFTA) and the North Atlantic Treaty Organization. It is a founding member of the Union for the Mediterranean. On 21 February 2003, Croatia submitted its application for full membership in the European Union (EU). On 18 June 2004 in Brussels, it was given the status of an official candidate for EU membership. The Stabilization and Association Agreement entered into force on 1 February 2005. On 30 June 2011, all thirty-five negotiating chapters were closed; this marked the formal closing of the negotiations for the accession of Croatia to the EU. The Accession Treaty was signed on 9 December 2011 in Brussels. At a referendum held on 22 January 2012, the citizens voted in favour of Croatia joining the EU. A total of 66.27% voted yes. Croatia became the twenty-eighth Member State of the EU on 1 July 2013.

§4. Population and Employment Statistics

7. In the 1990s, Croatia's socialist and semi-market economy was transformed into a system based on private property and open market. The problems stemmed from the fact that the transformation of ownership and privatization in the economy brought with them corruption and fraud. Economic progress was hampered by the years of war (1991–1995). Damage caused by the war was estimated at USD 37.1 billion in 1999.

8. The primary sector (agriculture, forestry and fisheries) employs 4.6% of the active population; the secondary sector (industry, construction, and mining) employs 24%, and the tertiary sector (services) employs 71.4% of the population (according to the 2023 data). Based on the data for total generated income, the leading industry is food, drinks and tobacco, followed by the chemical, oil, metal, paper and electrical equipment industry. Trade accounts for 20% of Croatia's Gross Domestic Product (GDP); about 15% of the workforce is employed in this sector. Tourism is a vital source of revenue for the state. In 2023, tourism brought in EUR 19.6 billion. According to the 2023 data, imports were worth EUR 40 billion, and exports were worth EUR 23 billion. In 2023, the GDP per capita was EUR 19,847. According to Eurostat, the Croatian GDP per capita in terms of purchasing power stands at 70.1% of the EU average.

9. According to the data of the Croatian Bureau of Statistics, in 2024, the active population in Croatia stood at 1,807,733. Out of that number, 1,722,892 persons were in employment. Broken down by gender, 801,768 persons (46.54%) were women. According to the Croatian Employment Service, the registered unemployment rate in 2024 was 4.8%. There has been a decrease in the registered unemployment rate. The labour surveys are carried out by the Croatian Bureau of Statistics, in line with the standard methodology proscribed by ILO and Eurostat; the data are therefore comparable internationally. According to the latest survey, in 2024, the ILO unemployment rate was 5.5%.

Table 1 Economically Active Population, Annual Average

	2021	*2022*	*2023*
Active population	1,712,653	1,736,096	1,772,443
Total persons in employment	1,575,837	1,619,969	1,663,522

	2021	*2022*	*2023*
Persons in paid employment in legal entities	1,362,169	1,402,240	1,439,796
Persons in employment in crafts and trades and freelancers[a]	194,861	199,072	205,309
Insured persons – private farmers[a]	18,807	18,657	18,417
Unemployed persons[b]	136,816	116,127	108,921
Registered unemployment rate,[c] per cent	8.0	6.7	6.1

[a] Registers of active insured persons taken over from the Croatian Institute for Pension Insurance.

[b] The Croatian Employment Service.

[c] The registered unemployment rate is calculated as the ratio of unemployed persons to the total active population (labour force).

Source: Croatian Bureau of Statistics, Statistical Information, 2024.

Table 2 Employment, Annual Average (Persons)

Activity Sector	*2022*	*2023*
Total	1,619,969	1,663,522
Agriculture	55,175	55,045
Agriculture, forestry and fishing	55,175	55,045
Industry	438,576	446,891
Mining and quarrying	3,977	3,982
Manufacturing	259,080	260,412
Electricity, gas, steam and air conditioning supply	14,574	14,547
Water supply; sewerage, waste management and remediation activities	26,368	26,629
Construction	134,577	141,321
Services	1,125,974	1,161,243
Wholesale and retail trade; repair of motor vehicles and motorcycles	234,581	239,819
Transport and storage	91,654	94,902
Accommodation and food service activities	114,742	122,362
Information and communication	57,727	62,647
Financial and insurance activities	38,105	37,237
Real estate activities	10,171	10,975

Activity Sector	*2022*	*2023*
Professional, scientific and technical activities	89,903	94,808
Administrative and support service activities	61,825	65,082
Public administration and defence; compulsory social security	115,138	117,559
Education	124,213	126,265
Human health and social work activities	117,781	117,176
Arts, entertainment and recreation	30,614	31,758
Other service activities	37,858	39,075
Activities of households as employers; undifferentiated goods – and services – producing activities of households for own use	1,662	1,578
Activities of extraterritorial organizations and bodies	–	–
Unclassified activities	244	343

Source: Croatian Bureau of Statistics, Statistical Information, 2024.

Table 3 Working Age Population, by Activity and Sex (in Thousands)

	2021	*2022*	*2023*
Working age population	3,508	3,508	3,266
Women	1,830	1,829	1,700
Labour force	1,816	1,835	1,707
Women	838	857	805
Persons in employment	1,678	1,707	1,603
Women	771	789	752
Unemployed persons	138	128	104
Women	67	68	53
Inactive population (15 and over)	1,692	1,673	1,559
Women	992	972	895
Activity rate (%)	51.8	52.3	52.3
Women (%)	45.8	46.9	47.3
Employment/population ratio (%)	47.8	48.7	49.1
Women (%)	42.1	43.1	44.2

	2021	2022	2023
ILO unemployment rate, (%)	8.0	7.9	6.6
Unemployment rate according to administrative sources (%)[a]	9.3	8.1	7.4

Source: Croatian Bureau of Statistics. The Labour Force Survey is based on international standards and is carried out by interviewing randomly selected private households. Since 2007, the Labour Force Survey has been carried out on a weekly basis. Data are calculated as an annual average of four quarters.

[a] Rates are calculated from the final administrative data.

Table 4 Persons in Employment, According to Activity Sectors and Average Hours Usually Worked, 2023

	Total (in thousands)		*Average Hours Usually Worked*	
	Persons in Employment	*Women*	*Total*	*Women*
Total	1,603	752	37.9	37.3
Agriculture	74	24	38.6	35.5
Industry	442	110	37.9	36.9
Services	1,079	605	37.8	37.4

Table 5 GDP of the Republic of Croatia

	2020	*2021*	*2022 (Provisional)*
GDP, market prices (current), million EUR	50,973	58,850	68,373
GDP, market prices (current), million USD	58,096	69,679	71,916
Population, mid-year estimate (in thousands)	4,047	3,949	3,857
GDP per capita, USD	14,354	17,643	18,648
Average annual exchange rate, HRK/USD	6,610754	6,363565	7,163295
Real growth rate (%)	-8.5	13.0	7.0

Source: Croatian Bureau of Statistics. Annual calculation GDP, *1995-2022, ESA 2010.*

Chapter 2. Definitions and Notions

§1. Labour Law

10. Labour law is defined in Croatia, just as it is in comparable legal systems, as a system of legal rules determining individual and collective employment relationships. The Labour Act of 2014 (last amended in 2023) applies to employment in the business sector, while the employment of civil servants is dealt with in the Civil Servants Act of 2023. Employment relationships in the private and public sector are considered to be part of labour law, although labour law as such recognizes some specific issues pertaining to civil servants (special aspects of the employment process, regarding the civil servants' disciplinary responsibility and of the termination of their employment). Self-employed persons are not protected by labour law; their contractual obligations are covered by the Obligations Act of 2005 (last amended in 2023). To sum up, the employees – subordinated persons who perform work for a salary – enjoy the protection of labour law.

I. Individual Labour Law

11. Individual labour law defines individual employment relationships. It includes the following areas: conclusion on an employment contract; temporary employment; protection of life, health and privacy of employees; trial period; education and training for work; working time; rest period and various forms of leave; protection of pregnant employees, parents and adoptive parents as well as carers of other dependent family members; protection of employees who are temporarily or permanently unable to work; salaries; inventions and technical innovations made by employees; prohibition of competition between an employee and their employer; compensation for the damage; and termination of an employment contract. The Labour Act guarantees a minimum level of legal protection to the employees in the business sector, while a higher protection standard is provided for by the relevant provisions in the employment regulations (*see* paragraph 28), collective agreements (*see* paragraphs 24–26 and 162–178), works agreements (*see* paragraph 27) or employment contracts (*see* paragraph 29).

II. Collective Labour Law

12. Collective labour law regulates the structure of industrial relations. It includes the following areas: establishment and registration of employees' and employers' associations; collective bargaining and collective agreements; strike and collective labour dispute resolution and the Economic and Social Council (a tripartite body whose purpose is to deal with economic and social issues and problems; for more details, *see* paragraphs 16 and 160). Ensuring workers' participation through works councils, employee meetings and employee representatives on the supervisory board and the board of directors (forms of employee participation) is a specific part of collective labour law. Furthermore, workers' participation is regulated by the Act on European Works Councils of 2014 (amended in 2017) and the Act on Workers Participation in Decision-Making in Societas Europaea and Societas Cooperativa Europaea of 2014. By these pieces of legislation, Croatia has transposed the Directives 2001/86/EC, 2003/72/EC, 2009/39/EC and 2015/1794 into national law. It is worth mentioning that there is a separate Act which, among others, regulates the representativeness of trade unions for collective bargaining and representativeness of employers' associations and trade unions in tripartite bodies: the Act on Representativeness of Employers' Associations and Trade Unions of 2014 (amended in 2015).

§2. Social Security Law

13. Croatia is defined as a welfare state by its Constitution. The rights in the area of social insurance and social protection are guaranteed by numerous laws. The pay-as-you-go compulsory pension insurance system is regulated by the Pension Insurance Act of 2013 (last amended in 2022). It provides for the following rights: old-age pension, early retirement pension, disability pension, survivors' pension, minimum pension, occupational rehabilitation, compensation allowance for physical injury, etc. The rights to a pension in the compulsory fully funded system are regulated in the following *leges specialis*: the Compulsory Pension Funds Act of 2014 (last amended in 2023) and the Voluntary Pension Funds Act of 2014 (last amended in 2023) and the Act on Pension Insurance Companies of 2014 (amended in 2023). The system of health insurance is regulated by the Mandatory Health Insurance Act of 2013 (last amended in 2023) and the Voluntary Health Insurance Act of 2006 (last amended in 2023), while unemployment insurance rights are guaranteed by the Act on Labour Market of 2018 (amended in 2023). The Act on Maternity and Parental Benefits of 2022 regulates a number of rights of pregnant workers and working parents. The Social Assistance Act of 2022 (last amended in 2023) is the *lex generalis* in the area of social assistance, and the Child Benefit Act of 2001 (last amended in 2023) is the *lex specialis* which provides for child benefits as a special right in the area of social assistance. Social security law is an area of public law, which means that administrative courts have jurisdiction over any disputes in this area of law.

Chapter 3. The Role of Government

§1. The Autonomy of Social Partners

14. Although the minimum levels of legal protection are defined in the Labour Act and in special laws (for instance, the minimum wage is regulated by the Minimum Wage Act of 2018, amended in 2021), the role of social partners in setting the working conditions cannot be overestimated. Freedom of association is enshrined in the Constitution of the Republic of Croatia and is defined in greater detail in the provisions of the Labour Act. The sheer number of provisions in the Labour Act regulating the employees' working conditions shows there is a need to define them in greater detail through collective agreements (and, subsidiarily, through employment regulations). According to the results of a survey conducted in December 2021, 46.5% of the employees in Croatia are covered by collective agreements *Source*: The Government of the Republic of Croatia, Draft of the Amendment to the Labour Act, July 2022.

§2. Government Institutions

15. The Croatian Employment Service keeps records of the unemployed, pays out unemployment benefits and implements active labour market policies. The State Inspectorate monitors the implementation of labour legislation. The Economic and Social Council, a tripartite body, plays an important role. *Inter alia*, it promotes the idea of trilateral cooperation involving the Government, trade unions and employers' associations. Its purpose is to solve economic and social issues and problems, encourage alternative means of dispute resolution in collective labour disputes and provide its opinions on the draft legislation in the area of labour and social security. There are also administrative bodies at the level of the counties and the City of Zagreb, which deal with labour affairs. One of their tasks is to receive the collective agreements applicable to their territory.

Chapter 4. Sources of Labour Law

§1. International and European Sources

16. According to Article 134 of the Constitution of the Republic of Croatia of 1990 (amended in 1997, 2000, 2001, 2010 and 2014), international agreements concluded and ratified in accordance with the Constitution and duly published are part of domestic legislation of Croatia and prevail over national laws. Their provisions may be changed or repealed only under the conditions and in the way specified therein or in compliance with the general rules of international law.

I. The International Labour Organizations

17. Croatia has been a Member State of ILO since 1992 and has ratified sixty-one ILO conventions (*source*: NORMLEX, 5 September 2024). Many of the ratified conventions were binding for Croatia while it was part of the Socialist Federal Republic of Yugoslavia. Croatia has ratified all of the eight core ILO Labour Conventions (conventions concerning fundamental workers' rights): Convention No. 87 on Freedom of Association and Protection of the Right to Organize, Convention No. 98 on the Right to Organize and Collective Bargaining, Convention No. 100 on Equal Remuneration, Convention No. 111 on Discrimination, Conventions on Child Labour No. 138 and No. 182, Convention No. 29 and Convention No. 105 on the Abolition of Forced Labour. The ILO Committee of Experts on the Application of Conventions and Recommendations in its recent reports has emphasized the issue of collective bargaining with yellow unions and excessive court delays in dealing with cases of anti-union discrimination. In the context of economic stabilization, according to the ILO Committee, priority should be given to collective bargaining as a means of determining the employment conditions of public servants rather than adopting legislation to restrain wages in the public sector. Furthermore, it makes a note of the unemployed Roma population, particularly women. In the Report on Application of International Labour Standards 2020, the Committee reiterates its request for the Government to take necessary measures to promote public awareness of the anti-discrimination legislation and the available remedies. For Freedom of Associations cases, *see* paragraph 152, where the issue is dealt with in greater detail. In its latest Report on Application of International Labour Standards 2024, the Committee noted that a considerable number of labour inspection positions in Croatia were still vacant; the Committee requested the Government to take the necessary measures to fill them as soon as possible and also to ensure that the number of labour inspectors is sufficient to secure the effective discharge of the duties of the inspectorate, including in the agricultural sector, and that workplaces are inspected as often and as thoroughly as is necessary to ensure the effective application of the provisions of Labour Inspection Conventions No. 81 and No. 129.

II. The Council of Europe

18. The European Social Charter, 1961, the Additional Protocol to the European Social Charter, 1988, and the Additional Protocol to the European Social Charter providing for a system of collective complaints were all ratified by Croatia in 2003. Croatia has accepted forty of the Charter's 72 paragraphs (Article 1 – the right to work, Article 2 – the right to just conditions of work, Article 5 – the right to organize, Article 6 – the right to bargain collectively, Article 7 – the right of children and young persons to protection, Article 8 – the right of employed women to protection, Article 9 – the right to vocational guidance, Article 11 – the right to protection of health, Article 13 – the right to social and medical assistance, Article 14 – the right to benefit from social welfare services, Article 16 – the right of the family to social, legal and economic protection, Article 17 – the right of mothers and children to social and economic protection), and 3 of the 4 articles of the Additional Protocol (Article 1 – the right to equal opportunities and equal treatment in matters of employment and occupation without discrimination on the grounds of sex, Article 2 – the right to information and consultation, Article 3 – the right to take part in the determination and improvement of the working conditions and working environment). Croatia has not made a declaration that would enable national NGOs to submit collective complaints. Dealing with one of the complaints (No. 116/2015, *Matica Hrvatskih Sindikata v. Croatia*), the Committee of Ministers has found a violation of Article 6(2) of the 1961 Charter. Namely, in this case, Croatia failed to promote collective bargaining.

§2. National Sources

I. Constitution

19. The Constitution, as the highest source of law, contains the basic tenets which are further enlarged upon in the relevant laws. It guarantees the right to work and to freedom of work as well as the right to form trade unions and employers associations. The Constitution also provides for possible restrictions on the right to organize trade unions in the armed forces and the police. Furthermore, it guarantees the right to strike (this right may be restricted by law in the armed forces, police, civil service and public services). It prohibits the employment of children under the age limit stipulated by law and guarantees the right to special health and safety protection for young people, mothers and disabled persons at work. Regular courts rarely invoke the provisions of the Constitution. However, the decisions of the Constitutional Court as sources of labour law are very important because the Constitutional Court of Croatia has several times quashed legal provisions on the basis of their unconstitutionality.

II. Ordinary Legislation

20. Until 1 January 1996, employment relations were regulated in the laws that were inherited from the socialist era. This situation prevailed until the entry into force of the Labour Act of 1995, which was modelled on the German protective labour legislation. Today, the Labour Act of 2014 (last amended in 2023) is in force. It has not introduced any substantial changes in relation to the structure of the Labour Act of 1995 apart from the introduction of provisions on work through digital platforms and regular amendments to the provisions to come in line with newly adopted EU directives. It is the *lex generalis* that regulates employment in Croatia unless otherwise specified by another law or treaty concluded, ratified and duly promulgated in accordance with the Constitution. The Labour Act of 2014 contains provisions on the conclusion of an employment contract; employment regulations; protection of life, health and privacy of employees; protection of pregnant employees, parents and adoptive parents; protection of employees who are temporarily or permanently unable to work; temporary employment; trial period, education and training for work; working time; rest period and various forms of leave; salaries and salary compensations; inventions and technical innovations made by employees; prohibition of competition between an employee and their employer; compensation for the damage; termination of an employment contract; exercise of the rights and obligations arising from employment; forms of employee participation; establishment and registration of the employees' and employers' associations; collective agreements; strike and collective labour dispute resolution; Economic and Social Council; work through digital labour platforms; administrative supervision of the application of labour regulations as well as the role of the labour inspection in such supervision; and penalties for violations committed by employers, trade unions and employers' associations. If there are any legal lacunae (*lacunae iuris*) in the Labour Act regarding the execution, effect and termination of an employment contract, a collective agreement or an agreement between the works council and the employer, the provisions of the Civil Obligations Act of 2005 (last amended in 2023) apply. In addition to the general law – the Labour Act of 2014 – there is also the Civil Servants Act, the Minimum Wage Act, the Occupational Health and Safety Act, the Act on Public Holidays in Croatia, the Maternity and Parental Benefits Act, the Act on Securing Debts Owed to Employees in Insolvency Proceedings, the Act on Labour Market, the Act on Occupational Rehabilitation and Employment of Persons with Disabilities, the Act on Suppression of Undeclared Work, the Act on the Representativeness of Employers' Associations and Trade Unions, etc. Since the Anti-Discrimination Act and the Gender Equality Act prohibit any discrimination in all spheres of public life, they contain provisions pertaining to employment discrimination. There are provisions relevant to employment relationships in the Civil Procedure Act, the Execution Act, the Bankruptcy Act, the Maritime Code and the Aliens Act. Furthermore, the Criminal Code of 2011 (last amended in 2024), in Articles 131 through 135, contains provisions on the following criminal offences: violation of the right to work, failure to pay salaries, abuse at work, violation of social security rights and unlawful employment.

III. Court Decisions

21. Apart from the Municipal Labour Court in Zagreb, there are no specialized courts to deal with labour disputes in Croatia. The amendments to the Law on the Territorial Jurisdiction and Seats of Courts of 2011 envisage the establishment of a specialized municipal labour court in Zagreb. The establishment of a special court which would deal with labour disputes has been justified by the fact that most of the labour-related lawsuits are heard by the Municipal Civil Court in Zagreb and the fact that this court has seen by far the greatest influx of such cases. The court in Zagreb adjudicates labour disputes as a Court of First Instance, while in the rest of Croatia, because there are no specialized labour courts, any labour disputes will be disposed of by the general jurisdiction municipal courts in the first instance. For the time being, there are no plans to establish an appellate labour court; appeals on the first instance judgments in labour cases are dealt with by the general jurisdiction county courts.

22. Although the Croatian legal system is not precedent-based, the importance of jurisprudence in the development of labour law cannot be underestimated. Abundant jurisprudence has established a list of just causes for the termination of an employment contract; the jurisprudence on the damages awarded for employment-related compensation claims is equally as voluminous.

IV. Collective Agreements

23. Collective agreements are an important source of labour law in Croatia. In the Croatian legal system, where many aspects of employment are regulated by peremptory provisions (*ius cogens*) in the labour legislation, collective agreements do not have the weight they do in (more flexible) legal systems which lack such norms. Despite the fact that the Labour Act guarantees in a number of coercive provisions the lowest level (minimum) of protection of the employees' rights, these regulations give the parties in a collective employment relationship enough leeway to provide for more favourable terms of employment through collective agreements and to define their relationship therein. According to the results of a survey conducted in December 2021, 46.5% of the employees in Croatia are covered by collective agreements (*source*: The Government of the Republic of Croatia, Draft of the Amendment to the Labour Act, July 2022). The prohibition to discriminate against employees on the basis of their membership in a trade union is interpreted by the courts in a way that the employers must not place employees who are not members of a trade union in a less favourable position than those who are trade union members, as regards their working conditions. This means that the normative provisions in a collective agreement apply to all the employees working for an employer bound by the collective agreement in question, regardless of whether they belong to the trade union which signed or acceded to the agreement. If the normative provisions in the collective agreement are breached by the employer, both the trade union members and non-members may have recourse to the courts to protect their rights stemming from the collective agreement. The trade unions are not content with this interpretation; they had managed to push through an amendment to the Labour Act compelling the employees who were not members of a trade union and who enjoyed the benefits of a collective agreement to pay a negotiation fee. The amendment was short-lived and was repealed as unconstitutional by the Constitutional Court in 2005 (for more details, *see* paragraph 177). The attempts of trade unions for legislative amendments aimed at differentiation in level of rights between unionized and non-unionized employees persist. The Amendment to the Labour Act of 2022 contained a provision guaranteeing a higher level of material rights to union members, i.e., it was possible to agree by a collective agreement the higher amount of jubilee award, Christmas bonus, holiday pay, severance pay due to retirement etc., for the employees who were trade union members, but not to all trade union members – solely to the members of the trade unions which were parties to the collective agreement. The Constitutional Court repealed in 2023 this provision as unconstitutional because it was in breach of the freedom of association.

24. Articles 192 through 204 of the Labour Act regulate the collective agreements. The provisions of the Act on Representativeness of Employers' Associations and Trade Unions are relevant in this context because they regulate the representativeness of trade unions for collective bargaining. This Act determines whether trade unions have the requisite level of representation for collective bargaining as well as stipulates the criteria to determine whether a higher-level trade union association is representative and may take part in the tripartite bodies at the national and local levels. *See* more in paragraph 165.

25. A collective agreement regulates the rights and obligations of the parties that have concluded it. It may also contain legal rules governing the conclusion, contents and termination of employment contracts, social security issues, and other issues arising from or related to employment. The legal rules contained in the collective agreement are directly applicable and binding on all persons who are subject to the collective agreement. A collective agreement may contain rules related to the composition and methods of work of the bodies authorized to conduct the amicable collective labour dispute resolution procedures. It is binding on all persons who have concluded it and on all persons who, at the time of the conclusion of such an agreement, were or subsequently became members of the association that is a party to the collective agreement. It must be concluded in written form. A collective agreement may have a fixed or indefinite duration. If it has a fixed duration, this period must not exceed five years. The termination of a collective agreement and the extension of the application of a collective agreement are also provided for in the Labour Act. The after-effect of a collective agreement is regulated by Article 199 of the Labour Act. In both cases: when the collective agreement has been terminated (and the termination period has expired) or when the period for which the collective agreement was concluded has expired, the legal rules contained in the collective agreement relating to its conclusion, the contents and termination of employment contracts continue to apply, as a part of previously concluded employment contracts, until a new collective agreement is concluded, in a period of three months. This period could be longer when the parties to the collective agreement stipulate it. This will be explained in greater detail below (*see* paragraphs 170–184).

V. Works Agreements

26. The works council may conclude a written agreement with the employer; it may contain legal rules governing employment matters. The agreement is directly applicable and binding on all employees employed with the employer who entered into it (Article 160(2) of the Labour Act). It may not regulate salaries, working hours and other matters which are, as a rule, regulated by a collective agreement, except when parties to a collective agreement have authorized the parties to the works agreement to do so.

VI. Employment Regulations

27. According to Article 26 of the Labour Act, any employer employing twenty or more employees is obliged to adopt and publish employment regulations regulating salaries, work organizations, the procedure and measures for the protection of employees' dignity, as well as anti-discrimination measures and other issues important for their employees, except when such issues are regulated by a collective agreement. Specific employment regulations may be adopted for undertakings or particular parts of a business enterprise or for particular groups of employees. The procedure for adopting employment regulations is stipulated in the Labour Act. Employers must consult the works council on the adoption of employment regulations. The works council may petition the competent court to invalidate the employment regulations or any provisions contained therein which are contrary to the law. If a works council has not been established, that right may be exercised by a trade union representative (shop steward). As this is a unilateral source of labour law (adopted by an employer), the trade unions want to see it repealed.

VII. Employment Contracts

28. Employment contracts are not only the foundation on which employment is based but also a source of law regulating the very substance of the employment relationship. As employment contracts often refer to collective agreements and employment regulations in their provisions (thus, for instance, some of the employment terms, such as the salary or annual leave, are defined by the relevant collective agreement or employment regulations), their importance as a source of law is somewhat reduced. They are considered a source of law when they define the employment terms in a manner more favourable than the collective agreements, employment regulations, works agreements and the law.

§3. THE HIERARCHY OF THE SOURCES OF LABOUR LAW

29. The principle *in favorem laboratoris,* contained in Article 9(3) of the Labour Act, is an exception to the usual hierarchy of sources, which gives the Constitution a greater legal force than the laws and bestows on the laws a greater legal force than on the by-laws. The provision prescribes as follows: 'If a right arising from employment is differently regulated in an employment contract, employment regulations, an agreement between the works council and the employer, a collective agreement or the law, the most favourable provisions shall apply to the employee, unless otherwise specified by the Labour Act or another Act.' The purpose of the *in favorem laboratoris* legal standard is to substitute a lower legal source for a higher one if the lower one is more favourable for the employees. The legal provision quoted above makes it clear that the *in favorem laboratoris* legal standard will fail to operate if the legislator has explicitly excluded the possibility.

Part I. Individual Employment Relationship

Chapter 1. Definitions and Concepts

§1. The Definition of Employee

30. The notion of 'employee' is defined in Article 4(1) of the Labour Act. An employee is a natural person who, in an employment relationship, carries out assignments for an employer. In the same provision, the legislator envisages that even members of the board of directors and executive officers may enter into an employment agreement; in other words, they are not outside of the scope of the concept. In practice, members of the board of directors and executive officers enter into employment contracts; few of them have civil law contracts, also known as managerial contracts. However, because members of the board of directors and executive officers assume the function of an employer, the legislator has stipulated that if they have employment contracts, they do not enjoy the protection of their labour rights related to the termination of the employment contract as envisaged by the Labour Act. For the same reason, they may not vote for or be voted to the works council. In addition to the specific features of the protection of labour rights related to the termination of the employment contracts of the members of the board of directors and executive officers, the legislator has also envisaged that the management personnel and the family members of an employer who are natural persons, who live in the same household as the employer, may agree to the working time, breaks and daily and weekly rest periods differently (more or less favourably) from the Labour Act which applies to other employees. The term 'management personnel' includes all the employees authorized to manage business operations of the employer who make decisions on the organization of the work and business of the employer (Article 88(3) of the Labour Act). This provision leads to the conclusion that the term 'management personnel' is broader than the term 'members of the board of directors and executive officers' in that it also includes the so-called middle management. In 2022, the provisions for digital labour platforms were introduced in the Labour Act. Among others, the provision on the facts on the basis of which the existence of an employment relationship can be assumed for those who work through digital labour platforms was introduced (Article 221.m(2)). These facts are as follows: (1) personal performance of remunerated work; (2) giving orders and instructions for the performance of work to a natural person within the framework of work organization and subordination of work; (3) limiting the freedom to refuse execution of the order or conditioning it with prohibited sanctions or other measures; (4) more detailed determination of the time, place and manner of performing work for a natural person, regardless of whether s/he uses his own means of work; (5) supervising the performance of work and monitoring the effects of a natural person in order to evaluate his/her work and the possibility of advancement; (6) prohibition of entering into transactions for one's own or another's account using the services of other platforms.

31. Civil servants are also considered employees; this means that the provisions of the Labour Act apply to their employment relationship unless the matter in question is regulated by the Civil Servants Act, decrees of the Croatian Government or other regulations passed in line with the Constitution, the law or collective agreements. Legal theory uses this provision as an argument to prove that the status of a civil servant is drawing closer to the status of employees in the business sector. However, the Civil Servants Act prescribes specificities in admission to the civil service and termination of employment of civil servants, as well as disciplinary procedures in case of their misconduct. It is worth mentioning that the civil servants and employees employed in state administration bodies do not conclude the employment contract but the head of the civil service issues decisions on admission to the civil service (which are unilateral acts).

32. The Labour Act prescribes the basic obligations and rights of employees and of employers arising from employment; these evince the substantial elements that distinguish an employment contract from a contract for service, which concerns the performance of specific work of an independent contractor as the contractual obligation. According to the Labour Act, the basic obligations of an employer are to assign an employee to a job and to pay them for the work they have performed. However, the basic obligation of an employee is to perform personally the job assigned, following the employer's instructions which are in line with the nature and type of work. Thus, the legislator abides by the universally accepted position in legal theory defining the essential elements of an employment relationship as the subordination of an employee to an employer, the remuneration due and the personal performance of the work.

§2. Kinds of Employment Contract

I. Contract for an Indefinite Period

33. The legislator has envisaged the conclusion of an employment contract for an indefinite period (open-ended employment contracts) as a rule. Although the Croatian Employment Bureau has warned that the number of fixed-term contracts has been on the increase over the past few years, open-ended employment contracts still prevail. According to Eurostat, temporary employees represent 14.1% of the total number of employees in Croatia in 2022. The EU average is 12%.

II. Fixed-Term Contract

34. As an exception, an employment contract may be concluded for a definite period ('fixed-term contract'). In that case, employment is determined by objective conditions such as reaching a specific date, completing a specific task, or the occurrence of a specific event. The contracting parties are very limited when concluding this contract because there is a need to justify it by providing a reason for its conclusion. Furthermore, a fixed-term employment contract can be concluded for a maximum duration of three years and the employer may not offer more than three successive fixed-term employment contracts to an employee for a continuous period longer than three years, except in order to substitute a temporarily absent employee, if this is necessary due to the completion of work on a project that includes financing from EU funds or if this is permitted by the law or a collective agreement in case of some objectively justified reasons. An interruption of service shorter than two months is not considered to be an interruption of the three-year period. If a fixed-term employment contract was concluded contrary to the provisions of the Labour Act or if an employee continued working for an employer after the expiry of the period originally covered by the contract, the employee is considered to have concluded an open-ended employment contract. The employer who employs a fixed-term employee must ensure that this employee enjoys the same working conditions as the employees who have an open-ended contract with the same employer or with an employer associated with him/her in line with special regulations. In that context, the employees are comparable if they have the same or similar qualifications and skills and perform the same or similar work. The employer is obliged to inform the employees who have fixed-term employment contracts about the available jobs for which they may apply and be offered open-ended employment contracts and provide them with further training and education under the same conditions as the employees working under open-ended employment contracts.

III. Part-Time Work

35. Less than 5% of the total number of employees in Croatia work part-time. A part-time employment contract is a contract of employment for the number of hours that falls short of the full working time, which may not exceed forty hours per week in Croatia. As is the case with employees who have fixed-term contracts, part-time employees must not work in conditions that are less favourable than those of full-time employees. A part-time employee may be employed by several employers at the same time. There is an exception to the maximum forty-hours working week. Namely, a full-time employee is allowed to conclude an employment contract with another employer for a maximum period of eight hours a week or up to 180 hours a year. Before starting work for another employer, the worker is obliged to inform current employer in writing about the concluded contract on additional work with the other employer. The current employer may claim the worker in a written form to stop performing additional work for another employer, if there are objective reasons for this, especially if it is against the statutory prohibition of competition or if it is performed within the worker's working time schedule at the current employer (about the statutory prohibition of competition, *see* more in paragraph 140). As regards the right of a part-time employee to a notice period or severance pay, the provisions of Article 62(4) of the Labour Act must be taken into account. According to this provision, if the previous length of service with the same employer is relevant for the acquisition of some rights, the period of part-time employment is considered equal to full-time employment. This means, for instance, that an employee who has been employed by the same employer for a year without any breaks in service will be entitled to at least one-month notice, regardless of whether they have worked full- or part-time (Article 122(1), related to Article 62(4) of the Labour Act). Likewise, two years of uninterrupted employment with an employer are one of the requirements for the acquisition of the right to severance pay. If other requirements for the payment of severance pay are met, an employee who has been working part-time will be entitled to severance pay after two years of uninterrupted service with an employer, same as a full-time employee (Article 126, related to Article 62(4) of the Labour Act). Again, Article 27(8) of the Pension Insurance Act of 2013 (last amended in 2022) stipulates that the period of part-time employment is considered full-time employment for the purposes of determining whether an employee meets the requirements necessary for the acquisition of the rights regulated in the Act. The scope of the rights and the requirements for the acquisition of these rights must be clearly distinguished here. The scope of the relevant right (the amount of the pension) is proportionate to the time spent in employment.

IV. Temporary Work

36. Agency work was made legal as late as 2003. The relevant provisions were incorporated into the Labour Act. Since then, 352 temporary work agencies have launched operations in Croatia. According to the Labour Act, a worker assignment contract between an agency and a user must be made in written form. In addition to the general provisions of the agency's business operations, the contract must also contain provisions on: (1) the number of assigned workers needed by the user undertaking, (2) the period for which the workers are assigned, (3) the place of work, (4) the jobs that will be performed by the assigned workers, (5) the method and period during which the user undertaking must submit the payroll accounts to the agency and the regulations applied by the user undertaking for the purpose of determining the salary, and (6) the person authorized to represent the user undertaking before the assigned workers. The contract may not be concluded for the purpose of: (1) replacing the employees of the user undertaking who are on strike, (2) performing works that were performed by the employees subject to the collective redundancy procedure effected by the user undertaking in a previous period of six months, (3) works that were performed by the employees whose contracts were terminated by the user undertaking in the last six months, due to business reasons, (4) jobs with reduced working hours because of the harmful effects on the employee's health and work capacity, (5) assigning employees to another agency. The agency may conclude a fixed-term or an open-ended employment contract for temporary work with a worker. This contract must also contain the provisions indicating: (1) that the contract is concluded for the purpose of assigning workers to the user undertaking temporary work, (2) the jobs to which the worker is assigned, (3) the agency's obligations towards the worker while they are assigned to the user undertaking. During the period when a worker employed by an agency is not assigned to a user undertaking, they are entitled to salary compensation. In order to evade their obligations towards the workers during the time when they are not assigned to users, the agencies often opt for the synchronization of the employment contracts and the worker assignment contracts. They enter into a temporary work employment contract whose duration is equal to the duration of the assignment of the worker to the user undertaking. The contract concluded for a fixed period of time that is equal to the period for which the worker is assigned to the user undertaking must contain provisions on: (1) the parties and their residence or seat, (2) the expected duration of the contract, (3) the user's seat, (4) the place of work, (5) the jobs that will be performed by the worker, (6) the date of commencement and termination of work, (7) the salary, salary supplements and the intervals in which the salary is to be paid, (8) the duration of a regular working day or week. The contracted salary may not be lower than the salary of an employee who is employed by the user undertaking. The same principle applies to all other working conditions of an assigned worker: they cannot be less favourable than the working conditions of an employee employed by the user undertaking. The agency may not assign a worker to the user to perform the same work for an uninterrupted period exceeding three years unless it is necessary for the purpose of replacing a temporarily absent employee or where it is allowed by the collective agreement on the grounds of some other objective reasons. A break shorter than three months is not considered an interruption of the three-year period of service.

§3. Special Groups of Employed Persons

I. Apprentices

37. An apprentice is defined in the Labour Act as a person employed for the first time in the occupation for which they have received schooling and who is trained for independent work in that occupation. After completing education, an apprentice/trainee is given an opportunity to gain hands-on experience and thus train for independent work. Apprenticeship is one of the reasons why a person may be offered a fixed-term contract. An employer may give an apprentice either a fixed-term contract or an open-ended contract. Under the Labour Act, the manner in which apprentices are to receive training for independent work must be regulated in the relevant employment regulations or an employment contract. A peculiarity of the employment of an apprentice lies in the fact that the employer may second the apprentice to work for another employer temporarily. The Labour Act as a general law regulating employment relationships stipulates the maximum length of the apprenticeship (one year), but there are special laws stipulating a longer duration of the apprenticeship (e.g., the apprenticeship lasts two years in courts, offices of state attorneys, and in notary-public offices but they can take the bar exam after eighteen months of apprenticeship). After completing the apprenticeship, an apprentice takes an occupational examination, if it is required by a law, another regulation, a collective agreement or employment regulations. The employer may terminate the employment of an apprentice who has not passed the occupational examination by an ordinary dismissal.

II. Juveniles

38. Persons under the age of 15 may not enter into employment; persons between the ages of 15 and 18 may not be employed if they are attending compulsory primary education. A minor older than 15 who has completed compulsory primary education may conclude an employment contract if they are empowered to do so by their legal representative. If a minor has been empowered by their legal representative to conclude a specific employment contract, this minor is considered to have the required legal capacity to conclude and terminate the contract and to carry out all the legal actions related to the fulfilment of the rights and obligations arising from or related to this contract. The legal representative may withdraw or limit the empowerment or terminate the employment on the minor's behalf. There is a prohibition on the employment of minors in specific jobs. A minor may not be employed in a job that may pose a risk to their health, morals or development. The labour minister has listed, in an ordinance, these jobs, as well as the jobs in which minors may work only after a medical examination, confirming that they meet the health requirements for these jobs. Where a minor, their parents or guardian, a works council, or a trade union have any doubts that the works performed by the minor will put his/her safety, health, morals or development at risk, they may request from the employer that an authorized physician performs a health assessment of the minor and provides his/her findings and opinion of whether the works performed by the minor indeed harm his/her safety, health, morals or development. Where it is established the works performed by the minor harm his safety, health, morals or development, the employer must offer the minor employee an employment contract for the performance of another appropriate job, and if there is no such job, the employer may terminate the minor's employment.

III. Disabled Persons

39. Croatia ratified the UN Convention on the Rights of Persons with Disabilities in 2007. It has also ratified ILO Convention No. 159 (Vocational Rehabilitation and Employment /Disabled Persons/ Convention, 1983). Seventeen per cent of the Croatian population is disabled, according to the data of the Croatian Public Health Institute in 2023. The high proportion of disabled persons in the population is a consequence, *inter alia*, of the Homeland War (1991–1995). In terms of legal norms, labour law affords disabled employees special protection. However, few disabled persons are actually in employment despite the quota system and the priority in the employment of qualified disabled job candidates. Namely, according to the Act on Occupational Rehabilitation and Rights of Persons with Disabilities of 2013 (last amended in 2020) and the Ordinance in the Establishment of a Quota for the Employment of Persons with Disabilities of 2018 (last amended in 2020), any employer who employs at least twenty employees is subject to the quota system. The quota is set at 3% of the total number of employees of the employer, regardless of the activity performed by the employer.

40. The Anti-discrimination Act of 2008 (as amended in 2012) prohibits, *inter alia*, any discrimination based on disability in all spheres of public life: this clearly includes work and employment. The same Act imposes an obligation on employers to provide reasonable accommodation for disabled persons in the workplace and in terms of their working conditions. A failure on the part of the employer to make adjustments to the working conditions and the workplace to accommodate a disabled person is considered discrimination. Exceptionally, such failure will not be considered discrimination if ensuring such accommodation would impose a disproportionate burden on the employer. Not only does the Labour Act prohibit discrimination, but it contains detailed provisions on the rights of employees who are unable to work, either temporarily or permanently. Thus, the legislator envisages the prohibition of dismissal if temporary incapacity is caused by an injury at work or an occupational disease, the prohibition of any detrimental effects on the promotion or the exercise of other rights after an employee has recovered from an injury at work or an occupational disease, and the right to return to the previous or another appropriate job of an employee who was temporarily unable to work. If an authorized person or body establishes that an employee has an occupational work incapacity or that he or she is in immediate danger of disability, the employer must, taking into consideration the expert opinion of the authorized person or body, offer the employee an employment contract for the performance of a job which they are able to perform and which must, to the greatest possible extent, correspond to the job previously performed by the employee. In order to provide such a job, the employer must adjust the work to the abilities of the employee, alter the working hours, and do all they can to provide an appropriate job to the employee. The employer may dismiss an employee who has occupational work incapacity or who is in immediate danger of disability only with the prior consent of the works council. An employee who has suffered an injury at work or has contracted an occupational disease and who is not given a job after the completion of the treatment and recovery is entitled to severance pay, which is at least double the one they would otherwise be entitled to. An employee who has unjustifiably refused to accept the offered job is not entitled to double severance pay. An employee who suffers an injury at work or an occupational disease is to be given precedence in occupational training and education organized by the employer.

The *lex specialis*, the Act on the Occupational Rehabilitation and Employment of Persons with Disability of 2013 (last amended in 2020), envisages a quota system for the employment of persons with disability and stipulates that priority should be given to the employment of persons with disability. These affirmative actions apply to all so-called big employers (those who employ at least twenty employees) except representations of foreign persons, foreign diplomatic and consular missions, integrative workshops and sheltered employment, employers in the textile, clothing, leather, wood and furniture production sectors, and newly established employers.

They are under an obligation to employ, in appropriate positions, subject to their own choice and under appropriate work conditions, 3% of persons with disabilities of the total number of employees they employ. The quota system does not apply to employers with less than twenty employees. In addition to the obligatory quotas, big employers must give precedence to disabled persons if they meet all the requirements stipulated in the vacancy advertisement. In case the employer fails to obey the above-explained quota system, there are substitute quotas, such as business cooperation with self-employed persons with disabilities or cooperation with sheltered workshops. The sanction for the failure to comply with the quota system is the payment of a monthly allowance in the amount of 20% of the minimum wage for each person with a disability (s)he was obliged to employ in order to meet the prescribed quota. Persons with a serious disability who cannot find a job on the open market can be employed in institutions and companies set up exclusively for them (sheltered employment). Disabled employees are guaranteed some rights in the pension insurance system. They are entitled to occupational rehabilitation and a disability pension under the conditions stipulated by the Pension Insurance Act.

41. According to the Mandatory Health Insurance Act of 2013 (last amended in 2023), if an employee is on sick leave for a continuous period of twelve months on account of the same illness, as well as when an employee incurs permanent work incapacity, they will be directed to undergo a work capacity and disability assessment, and will apply to the relevant body in the pension insurance system which carries out expert assessments; this body will then issue an assessment of their work capacity and disability, determining whether the insured person has incurred a general or occupational work incapacity. When the body in charge of issuing expert assessments determines that an insured person has incurred occupational work incapacity, it must list in its findings, opinion and assessment the jobs and assignments the insured person may perform in light of the determined residual work capacity and the jobs and tasks they cannot perform.

IV. Foreign Employees

42. Foreign nationals and stateless persons may be employed in Croatia only under the prescribed conditions stipulated in the following pieces of legislation: the Aliens Act of 2020, the Act on Citizens of Member States of the European Economic Area and their Family Members of 2019 (last amended in 2022) and the Act on Posting Workers to the Republic of Croatia and Cross-Border Enforcement of Decisions on Fines of 2020 (amended in 2022). According to the Aliens Act of 2020 (amended in 2022), aliens (third-country nationals) may work in Croatia if they possess a permit to reside and work or a work registration certificate (*see* paragraph 45). Some categories of aliens, defined by law, may be employed in the territory of Croatia without a permit because of their status or the nature and duration of the work they perform in the territory of Croatia. Third-country nationals who do not have a permit to reside and work or a work registration certificate may still work in

Croatia if they have the following: (1) temporary residence for the purpose of family reunification with a Croatian citizen, third-country national on long-term residence, permanent residence, granted asylum or subsidiary protection in accordance with the regulations governing international protection; (2) temporary residence for the purpose of a life partnership with a Croatian citizen, a third-country national on long-term residence, permanent residence, asylum or subsidiary protection in accordance with the regulations governing international protection; (3) temporary residence for the purpose of family reunification or life partnership with a third-country national who has been issued an 'EU Blue Card' or a residence and work permit for intra-corporate relocation; (4) temporary residence for the purpose of family reunification or life partnership with a third-country national holding a long-term residence permit in another European Economic Area (EEA) Member State; (5) temporary right to stay for humanitarian reasons; (6) autonomous residence; (7) temporary residence as a posted worker; (8) temporary stay for the purpose of research; (9) temporary residence for the purpose of family reunification or life partnership with a researcher; (10) temporary right to stay for the purpose of studying, if s/he works or is self-employed of a maximum of twenty hours per week, except when student internship is an integral part of the study program; (11) status of a full-time student when performing work through authorized intermediaries, without employment for a maximum of twenty hours a week; (12) temporary right to stay for the purpose of the stay of a long-term resident in another EEA Member State; (13) asylum or subsidiary protection or is an applicant for international protection in accordance with the regulations governing international protection; (14) long-term residence; (15) permanent residence. An employer who employs third-country nationals who are in Croatia illegally incurs very high fines. It is the employer who submits the application for the issuance of a permit to reside and work for the third-country national. However, before submitting it, s/he is obliged to request the implementation of the labour market test at the office of the Croatian Employment Service. The test determines whether there is an available person in the register of unemployed persons who meets the employer's requirements for employment or whether these requirements could be met by migrations of unemployed persons within Croatia. There is also an exception to the implementation of the labour market test. Namely, the Croatian Employment Service makes a decision on occupations for which the employer is not obliged to request the implementation of the labour market test. Primarily, these are occupations that are lacking in the national labour market.

43. Through the police administration or the police station in the place where a third-country national is residing or intends to reside, the Ministry of Internal Affairs decides on the issuing of the permit to reside and work. An appeal may not be filed against the decision, but the case can be brought before the Administrative Court. Through the police administration or the police station, the Ministry of Internal Affairs may refuse to issue the permit to reside and work if the employer is in breach of employment regulations, social security regulations, or tax obligations, bankruptcy or liquidation proceedings have been initiated for the employer, if the third-country national has failed to pay a fine imposed on them, if the employer has been convicted of criminal offences in the field of labour relations and social insurance, if the employer is sanctioned for undeclared work and/or illegal employment, etc. As a rule, the permit to reside and work is issued for the time period needed for the performance of the job or for the term of the employment contract; it may not exceed one year. As a derogation to the rule, the permit to reside and work can be issued with the term of validity of up to two years to a third-country national coming to work as an essential person in line with the Protocol of Accession of Croatia to the Marrakesh Agreement establishing the World Trade Organization. A permit to reside and work issued for the performance of seasonal work can be issued for a period of up to six months.

44. A work registration certificate allows aliens to work up to ninety or thirty days a year, depending on their jobs. A few examples: the certificates for up to ninety days a year may be issued to: service providers in tourism, tourist agents or entertainers; scientists; administrative staff, experts, teachers and lecturers at foreign cultural, educational and scientific institutions performing work in Croatia within the programme of cultural and educational cooperation; foreign correspondents and media reporters; artists, etc. The following categories may work up to thirty days a year: (1) those who carry out professional training or education of employees of legal and natural persons in Croatia; (2) employees of a foreign employer who is a manufacturer of machinery or equipment and who come for the delivery, installation or service, and their work is a condition for exercising warranty rights; (3) natural persons and employees of legal entities from third countries registered to perform funeral activities; (4) employees of the employer who exhibits at fairs or exhibitions; (5) third-country nationals employed in circuses and amusement parks, etc.

45. The Civil Servants Act of 2023 stipulates that Croatian citizenship is one of the requirements for employment in the civil service. However, a citizen of a Member State of the EEA or the Swiss Confederation who knows the Croatian language and the Latin alphabet can be admitted to certain positions in the civil service. A citizen of a third country can be admitted to certain positions in the civil service, with the prior approval of the state administration body responsible for official relations, if s/he knows the Croatian language and the Latin alphabet and has an approved residence, on the basis of which s/he can work without a residence and work permit. They can perform Information Technology (IT) tasks, general and administrative tasks, planning, material-financial and accounting tasks and similar tasks in state bodies. They can also work in auxiliary technical jobs in state bodies.

V. Posted Employees

46. The Labour Act regulates the mandatory contents of a written employment contract or a written certificate on the conclusion of an employment contract for posted workers working for a Croatian employer. Apart from the provisions contained in every employment contract, the contracts of employment for posted workers must contain additional provisions on: the duration of the work abroad; working time; paid non-working days and holidays; the currency in which the salaries are to be paid; other payments in cash and kind to which the employee will be entitled during the work abroad; link to a single national website on posting of workers to the Member State of the EU to which the worker is posted and the conditions of repatriation.

47. The rights of posted employees employed by a foreign employer are regulated by the Act on Posting of Workers to the Republic of Croatia and Cross-Border Implementation of the Decisions on Financial Penalties of 2020 (amended in 2022). It defines a posted employee as an employee posted by a foreign employer to carry out work for a limited period of time in Croatia, which is not a state in which a posted employee usually works. Posted employees are guaranteed the following working conditions: (1) the prescribed maximum working time and minimum rest periods; (2) the minimum paid annual leave; (3) the salary, including salary increments for overtime work; (4) health and safety at work; (5) measures protecting pregnant employees, employees who have recently given birth or are breastfeeding, and minors; (6) conditions of assignment through temporary employment agencies; (7) equal treatment of women and men and other protection against discrimination; (8) allowance or compensation for travel, food and accommodation costs during the performance of the task for which the employee was posted to Croatia provided that the domestic employee is entitled to such allowance or compensation based on the law or extended collective agreement; (9) the quality of accommodation to the extent to which the domestic employee is entitled, if the employer is obliged by law or the extended collective agreement to provide accommodation to domestic employee who is absent from his/her usual place of work. About the extension of the application of the collective agreement, *see* more in paragraph 184. The same guarantees extend to the posted employees assigned through temporary employment agencies. However, when the working conditions are more favourably regulated by the law of the state of residence of the foreign employer and which applies to the employment of the posted worker than by the law of Croatia, the posted worker is entitled to a more favourable right.

VI. Pregnant Employees/Parents

48. The Labour Act prohibits employers from refusing to hire a pregnant woman and from terminating her employment contract. A pregnant woman may not be offered an amended employment contract, except if her current job poses a risk to her life or health or the life and health of her child. In that case, if the employer is unable to offer the pregnant woman another job, the employee is entitled to paid leave financed by the employer. Needless to say, this provision, which imposes a financial burden on employers, has not made it easier for women to find work. The Gender Equality Ombudswoman has repeatedly warned in her annual reports of the fact that women are unlawfully offered fixed-term contracts, which are not renewed if they fall pregnant. According to the Labour Act, if the prior duration of employment entitles the employee to specific rights arising from employment or related to employment, the periods of maternity and parental leave are to be considered full-time work. During pregnancy, maternity and parental leave, while a parent or adoptive parent exercises their right to shorter working hours, during adoption leave and leave granted to parents caring for a child with serious developmental problems, and in the fifteen days after the cessation of pregnancy or the cessation of the period during which these rights are exercised, the employer may not dismiss from work a pregnant woman or a person exercising one of these rights. However, during the liquidation procedure (when the employer ceases to operate), their contracts of employment can be terminated due to business-related reasons. The prohibition of the termination of an employment contract, including for reasons not related to the pregnancy or taking the rights protecting parenthood which remains in force for as long as the rights protecting parenthood are exercised (it must be noted that some may be exercised for years) does not contribute to the employment of women.

Taking into account the long duration of compulsory maternity leave, which lasts ninety-eight days, one concludes that the legislator fails to understand that excessive protection of women results in discrimination against them in the labour market. After the expiry of maternity and parental leave, adoption leave or part-time work, the employee who has exercised any of these rights has the right to be assigned to the same job they performed before exercising this right, and if the need for such job no longer exists, the employer is obliged to offer them an employment contract for the performance of another appropriate job, under the conditions which are not less favourable than the conditions of the job the employee performed before exercising the right in question.

49. In addition to the Labour Act and its provisions on the protection of pregnant employees and parents, there is the Maternity and Parental Benefits Act of 2022. The purpose of the law is to protect maternity, care for a newborn baby, child-raising and upbringing and to reconcile work and family life. This law contains, among others, regulations on maternity, paternity and parental leave (*see* further in paragraphs 83–85).

Chapter 2. Duties of the Parties in the Course of the Employment Relationship

§1. Duties of the Employee

I. Duty to Work

50. An employee has the duty to perform the job personally and may not confer the duty to work to another person. An employer has decided to employ a specific person and wants that person to perform the job specified in the employment contract because of the specific skills and other personal qualities. An employer has concluded an employment contract with an employee because of their qualifications (because they meet the requirements for the employment) and is entitled to demand from that employee (and not from their replacement or assistant) to perform the job. Exceptionally, when an employee has been temporarily rendered unable to perform the job (e.g., if they are on sick leave for health reasons), the employer may assign another person to perform the job the employee has undertaken to perform in the employment contract. The employer has concluded the employment contract with the employee for the performance of specific jobs and may not demand the employee to perform other tasks. If there is no longer any need to perform the tasks specified in the initial employment contract, the contract may be terminated, and the employee may be offered another employment contract specifying other tasks. In the performance of their job, employees must comply with the instructions and subject to the supervision of the employer.

II. Ancillary Duties

51. Employees are prohibited from damaging the employer's property. An employee who, at the workplace or in relation to work, either intentionally or due to gross negligence, causes the employer to suffer damage is obliged to compensate the employer for such damage. If the damage has been caused by several employees, each employee is liable for part of the damage caused by them. If it is impossible to determine which part of the damage was caused by which employee, all the employees are considered to be equally liable and have to compensate for the damage in equal parts. If several employees have caused damage in the course of the commission of a premeditated criminal offence, they are jointly liable for the damage caused. If determining the amount of the damage would cause disproportionate costs, the amount of compensation for the damage for some harmful acts may be determined in advance. The harmful acts and compensation have to be provided for in a collective agreement or employment regulations. If the damage caused by a harmful act is much greater than the predetermined amount of compensation, the employer may claim compensation for the amount of the damage actually suffered and established. An employee who, at the workplace or in relation to the work, either intentionally or due to gross negligence, causes damage to a third party for which compensation has been paid by the employer must compensate the employer to the amount the employer paid to the third party. Collective agreements or employment regulations may establish the conditions and methods for reducing the damage compensation or exempting an employee from the obligation to pay such compensation.

52. The Occupational Health and Safety Act of 2014 (last amended in 2018) provides for some additional obligations of the employees. Smoking is prohibited in working areas except where the employer has exceptionally determined that smoking is allowed in a special room. The employee must not be under the influence of alcohol or other addictive substances during work and to bring them into the workplace.

53. Employers can prohibit employees from disclosing their trade secrets. According to the Act on the Protection of Undisclosed Information with Market Value of 2018, a trade secret holder (an employer) can regulate the handling of trade secrets by his/her internal rules. Anyway, in line with Article 3(1)(c) of the Directive (EU) 2016/943 on the protection of undisclosed know-how and business information (trade secrets) against their unlawful acquisition, use and disclosure, the acquisition of a trade secret is lawful when it is obtained by the exercise of the right of workers or workers' representatives to information and consultation in accordance with separate legislation and Union law.

54. The Labour Act provides for the statutory and contractual prohibition of competition of the employees with their employer. *See* further in paragraphs 140 and 141.

§2. Duties of the Employer

I. Duty to Pay Remuneration

55. Article 90 of the Labour Act defines the manner in which salaries are determined for employees in the business sector. An employer bound by a collective agreement must not calculate and pay the employee remuneration lower than the amount set by the collective agreement. If the basis and criteria for salaries have not been established by a collective agreement, an employer employing twenty employees or more must set them in the employment regulations. If the salary has not been established by such methods and the employment contract does not contain sufficient data for its establishment, the employer is obliged to pay the employee an appropriate salary. An appropriate salary is a salary regularly paid for equal work, and if it is impossible to establish such a salary, then the employer must pay the salary established by the court after taking into account the circumstances. To summarize, a collective agreement is the primary legal source for the determination of the employees' salaries in the business sector. The employment regulations and employment contracts are subsidiary sources. However, the salaries of employees in public services are determined by the Act on Salaries in Civil Service and Public Services of 2023. According to this Act, the basic salary in public services is determined by a collective agreement concluded by the Government of

Croatia and the public services trade union. If no such collective agreement has been signed before the adoption of the state budget of Croatia for the following year, the basic salary for public services is set by the Government of Croatia in a separate decision.

56. Salaries paid to the employees in Croatia must not be lower than the minimum wage defined by law. The Minimum Wage Act of 2018 (last amended in 2024) sets the minimum wage, the manner in which this amount is adjusted and the fines payable by the employers who fail to pay the minimum wage in line with the Act. The Act defines the minimum wage as the lowest monthly gross salary payable to an employee working full-time. The amount is set once a year, no later than 31 October of the current year, for the following calendar year. It cannot be determined in an amount less than the amount determined for the previous year. The Minister of Labour, after consultation with the social partners, proposes to the Government of Croatia the amount of the minimum wage. When making this proposal, the Minister of Labour needs to take into account the increase in the share of the minimum wage in the average gross salary paid to the legal entities from January to July of the current year, inflation, salary developments, unemployment and employment, demographic trends, productivity trends and the overall state of the economy. Apart from this, the Minister of Labour needs to pay special attention to the activities with low salaries and vulnerable groups of employees. The gross amount of minimum wage for 2025 in Croatia is set at EUR 970.

57. According to the Labour Act, the salary is due after the work has been performed. It must be paid in money at intervals, not exceeding one month. Unless otherwise specified by a collective agreement or employment contract, the salary for the previous month must be paid no later than the fifteenth day of the current month. When paying a salary, salary compensation or severance pay, the employer must give the employee a payroll account, clearly showing how the salary, salary compensation or severance pay were calculated. The employer who fails to pay a salary, salary compensation or severance pay when they are due, or who fails to pay them in full, must provide the employee with a payroll account stating the amount owed by the end of the month in which the salary, salary compensation or severance pay were due. The payroll accounts are valid as writs of execution. It must be noted that failure to pay salaries is one of the just causes allowing the trade unions to call for a strike: according to Article 205(1) of the Labour Act, trade unions have the right to call for a strike, *inter alia*, on the grounds of non-payment of salary or salary compensation.

58. According to the Labour Act, an employee is entitled to an increase in salary because of arduous working conditions, for overtime and night work, and for work on Sundays, holidays, and other days that are not working days according to the law. An employee has the right to salary compensation for periods in which they did not work for a justifiable reason established by the law, other regulations or a collective agreement.

59. The employer must not, without the consent of the employee, settle their claim against the employee by withholding the payment of salary or part of salary or by withholding the payment of salary compensation or part of salary compensation. Employees may not give their consent in advance before the claims arise. The protection of salary if it is withheld without consent is regulated by the Execution Act of 2012 (last amended in 2024). For more details, *see* paragraph 91.

60. The Criminal Code of 2011 (last amended in 2024) contains in its Article 132 the criminal offence of non-payment of salary. This provision envisages a prison sentence of up to three years for a person who fails to pay the salary to an employee. The same sanction is envisaged for those who fail to provide data or who provide inaccurate data for the calculation of salaries in order not to pay salaries or to pay them in part. The criminal offence of the failure to pay salary did not occur if the salary was not paid because the employer was unable to access the funds in their account or due to the lack of funds in the employer's account not caused by the intent to evade the payment of the salary. If the person who has committed the offence of failure to pay salary later pays the salary in arrears, the court may decide not to impose any sanctions.

61. According to the data from the Croatian Bureau of Statistics, the average gross salary in Croatia in November 2024 was EUR 1,900; the average net salary in November 2024 was EUR 1,366.

62. According to recent Croatian Bureau of Statistics data in2023, women's gross hourly earnings were on average 6.8% below those of men in Croatia, although, according to the EU law, Labour Act and ILO Convention No. 100 ratified by Croatia, an employer must pay equal salaries to women and men for equal work and for work of equal value. According to the Gender Ombudsperson, in certain sectors (such as the healthcare and social assistance sector and financial and insurance sector), the gender pay gap is almost 26% as a consequence of the glass ceiling. For more details about equal pay, *see* paragraphs 93 and 94.

II. Duty to Employ the Employee

63. The obligation to employ exists when the legislator has envisaged affirmative actions in order to ensure the employment of the underrepresented groups in the labour market. The obligation of the so-called big employers to employ disabled persons has already been discussed above (in the chapter 'Disabled Persons'). There is a similar obligation regarding the employment of ethnic minorities (under the Constitutional Act on the Rights of Ethnic Minorities of 2002, last amended in 2011, a Plan of the Employment of Ethnic Minorities in Civil Service and Public Administration Bodies must be adopted, covering a specific time period) and of the underrepresented gender. Under the Gender Equality Act of 2008 (last amended in 2017), the public administration bodies and legal persons in which the state has a majority stake must apply affirmative actions and adopt action plans for the promotion and establishment of gender equality. The purpose of affirmative actions is to promote equal participation of women and men in legislative, executive and judicial bodies, including public services, and to gradually increase the participation of the underrepresented sex in order for its representation to be equal to its percentage in the total population of Croatia. The implementation of affirmative actions is allowed if one sex is substantially underrepresented, i.e., if one sex is represented with less than 40% in political and public decision-making bodies. When making appointments to diplomatic offices, boards, commissions and delegations representing Croatia at the international level, public bodies must seek to ensure the balance in terms of the representation of women and men.

64. When a court judgment finds that an employee has been unlawfully dismissed and that there is an obligation to re-employ them, this does not constitute the duty to employ; in effect, the court judgment finds that the employment has never been terminated.

III. Duty of Equal Treatment

65. The Constitution of the Republic of Croatia in Article 14 prohibits discrimination based on any characteristic whatsoever (this is an open-ended clause). More specifically, according to that provision, all persons in Croatia shall enjoy the same rights and freedoms, regardless of race, colour, gender, language, religion, political or other conviction, national or social origin, property, birth, education, social status or other characteristics. However, the Anti-discrimination Act of 2008 (amended in 2012) provides an exhaustive list of the grounds of discrimination. Pursuant to Article 1(1), it is prohibited to discriminate against a person on any of the following seventeen grounds of discrimination: race or ethnic affiliation or colour, gender, language, religion, political or other belief, national or social origin, property, trade union membership, education, social status, marital or family status, age, health condition, disability, genetic heritage, native identity, expression and sexual orientation. This Act prohibits discrimination in all areas of social life, including the area of employment and working conditions. It prohibits both direct and indirect discrimination, harassment, sexual harassment, victimization, failure to make reasonable accommodation, encouragement of discrimination, associative discrimination and segregation. The purpose of the Anti-discrimination Act of 2008 was to bring the Croatian anti-discrimination legislation in line with the EU *acquis*. Therefore, the whole concept of non-discrimination (definitions of the forms of discrimination, exceptions to the prohibition of discrimination, the burden of proof in anti-discrimination cases, etc.) has been adopted from the relevant EU directives. The Anti-discrimination Act of 2008 set up the Ombudsman as a central body responsible for the suppression of discrimination. In addition to the Ombudsman, there is an Ombudsman for Gender Equality, an Ombudsman for Persons with Disability and an Ombudsman for Children. The Anti-discrimination Act of 2008 lists special legal actions designed to protect persons against discrimination: a lawsuit to determine the existence of discrimination, a lawsuit to prohibit or eliminate discrimination and a lawsuit for pecuniary and moral damages. The ruling finding that the right to equal treatment has been violated could also be published in the media at the respondent's cost if so requested by the claimant. The major problem in this area of law is not the inappropriate legislation but the lack of case law, which is the result of the fact that the persons discriminated against are not familiar with the anti-discrimination legislation and their rights. This has led to criticism of Croatia by the UN Committee on the Elimination of Discrimination against Women. The length of litigation has also deterred persons who have suffered discrimination from bringing their case before the court.

66. The Constitutional Court of Croatia repealed in several cases the discriminatory provisions in various acts. Thus, for instance, the Court found that the fact that men and women faced different age requirements for old-age pension constituted gender discrimination. Under the repealed provision of the Pension Insurance Act, women were able to retire five years earlier than men. In line with the Constitutional Court's decision, the legislator has envisaged a gradual increase in the age limit for retirement for women; the retirement requirements for women and men will be equalized in 2030.

67. In addition to the Anti-discrimination Act of 2008 (amended in 2012), which is the *lex generalis* prohibiting discrimination, a number of special laws contain provisions with the same effect (Gender Equality Act, Same-Sex Partnership Act, and Civil Servants Act). The Labour Act also contains a provision for the protection of the employees' dignity, which protects them from harassment and sexual harassment as specific forms of discrimination (Article 134). According to that provision, an employer employing at least twenty employees is obliged to appoint a confidential counsellor and an employer who employs more than seventy-five employees is obliged to appoint two persons of different genders who, in addition to him, are authorized to receive and resolve complaints related to the protection of employees' dignity. Confidential counsellors can be employees or persons who are not employed by the employer. These are persons who are, in addition to the employer, authorized to receive and deal with the complaints related to the protection against harassment and sexual harassment. The employer and the confidential counsellor are obliged, within the time limit prescribed by a collective agreement, an agreement between the works council and the employer or employment regulations, and not later than eight days from the day when the complaint is filed, to consider the complaint and take all the necessary measures appropriate for a particular case, to stop the harassment or sexual harassment, if they have established that harassment has occurred. If the employer has failed to take measures to prevent harassment or sexual harassment within that time limit, or if the measures taken by them are clearly inappropriate, the employee who is a victim of harassment or sexual harassment has the right to stop working until they have been offered protection, if they bring an action within the next eight days in the competent court. If the circumstances indicate that it is improbable to expect that the employer will protect an employee's dignity, the employee is not obliged to file a complaint with the employer and has the right to stop working, provided that they bring an action in the competent court and notified the employer thereof, within eight days of the date when they stopped working. During the period off work, the employee is entitled to salary compensation in the amount they would have received if they had actually worked. However, if it is established by a final court decision that the employee's dignity has not been violated, the employer can demand the return of the paid salary compensation. The Anti-discrimination Act of 2008 (amended in 2012) prescribes penalties for misdemeanours caused by harassment, sexual harassment and victimization.

Chapter 3. Working Time, Public Holidays and Annual Leave

§1. Working Time

68. Working time (full-time, part-time, reduced), overtime, working time scheduling and rescheduling, night work, and work in shifts have been dealt with in the provisions of the Labour Act (Articles 60 through 72) in a very rigid manner, which has made it very difficult to organize working and resting time efficiently. According to Article 60 of the Labour Act, working time is a period of time during which an employee is obliged to carry out tasks or during which they are ready (available) to carry out tasks at the workplace or another place defined by the employer following the employer's instructions. The period of time during which an employee must stand ready to respond to the call of the employer to perform tasks is not considered working time if the employee is not at his or her workplace or another place defined by the employer. On-call duty and the allowances for this time are determined in the employment contract or collective agreement. The time an employee spends performing tasks after being called in by the employer is considered working time, regardless of whether the tasks are performed at the place defined by the employer or at the place chosen by the employee.

69. An employment contract may be concluded for full-time or part-time work. Full-time work must not exceed forty hours a week. Full-time work may cover less than forty hours a week if it is so specified by a law, a collective agreement, an agreement between the works council and the employer or an employment contract. It is worth mentioning that a full-time employee is allowed to conclude an employment contract with another employer for a maximum period of eight hours a week or up to 180 hours a year. Before starting work for another employer, the employee must inform current employer(s) in writing about the concluded contract on additional work with the other employer. The current employer(s) can ask the employee in writing to stop performing additional work at another employer, if there are objective reasons for this, especially if it is against the statutory prohibition of competition or if it is performed within the employee's working time schedule at the current employer, i.e., at the employer or the employers with whom the employee already has a concluded employment contract. Part-time work is defined as working time shorter than full-time work. The employees who work part-time must have the same working conditions as their full-time counterparts. An employee may enter into part-time employment contracts with several employers at the same time, but the total working time must not exceed the maximum full-time working week. When entering into a part-time employment contract, the employee is obliged to inform the employer about the part-time employment contracts he or she already has with another employer or employers. If the previous duration of employment with the same employer is relevant for the acquisition of a right, the period of part-time employment is considered full-time employment. The employer must consider an application submitted by an employee who has a full-time employment contract to conclude a part-time employment contract and likewise an application by an employee who has a part-time employment contract to conclude a full-time employment contract if there are possibilities for such work with the employer.

70. In addition to full-time and part-time work, there is a reduced working time. The Labour Act defines the requirements for reduced working time: working time is reduced in proportion to the harmful effect of the working conditions on the employee's health and working capacity in those jobs where, despite all the occupational safety and health measures, it is impossible to protect the employee from harmful effects. Such jobs, as well as the actual working time, are defined in special regulations. If they are not defined in that way, the Minister of Labour, at the proposal of a person who may be a party to a collective agreement under the Labour Act and with the prior consent of the minister responsible for health, must adopt an ordinance to regulate these issues. The working time of employees in such jobs must not exceed the working time established by a special regulation/ordinance. These employees must not accept additional employment in a similar job with another employer. A collective agreement or an employment contract may stipulate that an employee who does not work full-time in such jobs may do other work part-time, but these other jobs must not be harmful to the employee's health, and the total working time must not exceed the full-time limit. As regards the exercise of the right to a salary and other rights arising from employment or related to employment, reduced working time is considered to be equal to full-time work. If daily and weekly work schedules are not regulated by a law, a collective agreement, an agreement between the works council and the employer or an employment contract, the work schedule is determined by the employer in a written decision. The employer must notify the employees about the work schedule or changes to the schedule at least one week in advance, except in cases of emergency overtime work. Where the working time is not distributed evenly by weeks, the maximum number of hours per week is fifty, including overtime work (or sixty hours per week, including overtime work if it is so agreed by the contracting parties of a collective agreement). When the working time is unevenly distributed, the employee may not, in any period of four successive months, work more than forty-eight hours a week on average, including overtime work.

The work schedule for employees who are legal minors must not exceed eight hours a day. Where this is dictated by the nature of work, full-time or part-time work may be rescheduled in such a way that in the course of twelve continuous months, there may be a period of time with more working hours and a period of time with less working time than full-time or part-time work, provided that the average working time during this period does not exceed the regular full-time or part-time working hours. Where work time rescheduling is not provided for in a collective agreement or an agreement concluded between the works council and the employer, the employer must set a plan for the rescheduled working time indicating the jobs and the number of employees included in the scheme. The employer must submit the rescheduled plan to a labour inspector. The rescheduled working time is not considered overtime. If working time is rescheduled, it cannot exceed forty-eight hours a week (this includes overtime) in the period when the working hours are longer than the regular full-time or part-time limit. As an exception, the rescheduled working time may exceed forty-eight hours a week to a maximum of fifty-six hours a week for regular work or sixty hours a week for seasonal work, provided there are regulations to that effect in a collective agreement and provided the employees submit a written statement giving their consent to perform such work to the employer.

An employee who refuses to work for more than forty-eight hours a week while the rescheduled working time is in effect must not suffer any adverse effects as a result of their refusal. The period when hours are longer than regular full-time or part-time work may not exceed four months during the period when working time is rescheduled unless otherwise provided in a collective agreement, in which case it cannot exceed six months. Legal minors are prohibited from working longer than eight hours a day while the rescheduled working time is in effect.

Pregnant employees, parents of children under three years of age, single parents of children under six years of age or part-time employees may work overtime only if they submit to the employer a written statement indicating their consent to such work, except where there is force majeure.

§2. Overtime

71. Overtime is regulated in Article 65 of the Labour Act. In case of force majeure, an extraordinary increase in the scope of work and in other similar cases of absolute necessity, the employee is obliged, at the employer's request, to work longer than full-time working hours, but the total working time of the employee may not exceed 50 hours a week. Overtime work for each individual employee must not exceed 180 hours a year unless otherwise provided for in the collective agreement, in which case it may not exceed 250 hours a year. 'Overtime work by legal minors is prohibited. Pregnant employees, parents of children under three years of age, single parents of children under six years of age or part-time employees may work overtime only if they provide a written statement of their consent to such work, except where there is force majeure.'

§3. Night Work and Shift Work

72. Night work is defined in Article 69 of the Labour Act as any work between the hours of 10 pm and 6 am of the next day or, in agriculture, between 10 pm and 5 am of the next day. It is possible to regulate night work differently from the Labour Act by another act or regulation, a collective agreement or an agreement between the employer and the works council. Since the legislator provides for special protection of legal minors, their night work is defined in a more protective way. For minors employed in the industry, work between the hours of 7 pm and 7 am of the next day is considered night work. For minors employed in other sectors, work between the hours of 8 pm and 6 am of the next day is considered night work. A night employee is defined as an employee whose work schedule compels him to work in the course of a single day for at least three hours during the hours defined as night or who, in the course of a calendar year, works at least one-third of his working time during the hours defined as night. In the period of four months, a night employee is not allowed to work more than eight hours a day on average in any twenty-four-hour period. An employer may not order a pregnant employee or an employee who has given birth or an employee who is breastfeeding to do night work during pregnancy and in the period of up to one year of the child's life, provided that she presents a certificate of her pregnancy or a certificate on breastfeeding or a duly authorized physician has assessed that such work will not endanger her life or the life or health of the baby (Article 24(6) of the Act on Maternity and Parental Benefits). Night work is prohibited for minors unless such work is a pressing need in business activities regulated by special legislation and where it may not be performed by adult employees. In such cases, night work must not last longer than eight hours within a period of twenty-four hours, and minors must not work in the period from midnight to 4 am. Minors may only perform night work under the supervision of an adult person.

73. According to Article 71 of the Labour Act, shift work is a method of organizing work at an employer's workplace whereby employees take turns in the same job and at the same workplace in accordance with a work schedule, which may be continuous or discontinuous. A shift employee is defined as an employee who works for an employer who has put in place a shift work pattern; shift employees perform their job in different shifts over a period of one week or one month. If work is organized in shifts, a rotation of shifts must be ensured so that employees work consecutive night shifts for no more than one week. The employer has some obligations towards night and shift employees. When the employer organizes night or shift work, they must make an effort to adjust the work schedule to the needs of the employees and take into account the safety and health requirements in line with the nature of work performed during night or shift work. The employer must provide safety and health protection for the night and shift employees in line with the nature of work they perform, including safety and protective equipment that is relevant and required for all other employees. Night employees are entitled to regular medical check-ups. The cost of medical check-ups is borne by the employer. If the medical check-ups indicate that a night employee suffers health problems as a result of night work, the employer must ensure that the employee is assigned a work schedule that will allow them to perform their job at other times, i.e., not at night. If it is not possible, the employer must offer the employee an employment contract for the performance of tasks outside the night work hours, which they are capable of performing. These tasks must, to the largest extent possible, correspond to the tasks the employee was assigned earlier.

§4. Work on Sundays and Public Holidays

74. The right to a weekly rest and to annual leave is guaranteed by Article 55(3) of the Constitution of the Republic of Croatia, as follows: 'Each employee shall be entitled to a weekly rest and annual leave with pay, and shall never waive these rights.' More detailed provisions on the right to a weekly rest and annual leave (*see* paragraph 78) are contained in the Labour Act. According to Article 75 of the Labour Act, a weekly rest lasting at least twenty-four consecutive hours plus the hours of daily rest is taken on Sundays and on the day immediately preceding or following Sunday. A minor is entitled to a weekly rest of continuous duration of no less than forty-eight hours. Where an employee may not exercise the right to a weekly rest in the way described above, they are entitled to compensatory weekly rest right after their working time with no weekly rest or with a shorter period of rest. Exceptionally, the employees who work in shifts and who cannot take their weekly rest because of technical reasons which constitute an objective necessity or because of the work organization may take their weekly rest as a continuous period of at least twenty-four hours, not counting their daily breaks.

75. The implementation of the provisions of the Labour Act regarding working time, breaks, and daily and weekly rest periods may be restricted for some categories of employees: such restrictions may be agreed upon with the employer for management personnel and for employees who are family members of an employer who is a natural person provided they live in the same household as the employer. The provisions on working time, breaks and daily and weekly rest will not apply to these categories of employees if the employer and the employees have agreed on that.

76. The Act on Public Holidays in the Republic of Croatia of 2019 envisages thirteen holidays, i.e., paid days off.

§5. Annual Leave

77. The Labour Act guarantees the right to paid annual leave of at least four weeks in each calendar year. Employees who enjoy special protection (i.e., employees with disability, minors and employees who perform jobs where they cannot be protected against harmful effects despite the application of occupational safety and health measures) are entitled to at least five weeks of paid annual leave per each calendar year. A longer annual leave and the number of working days which are calculated as annual leave can be established by a collective agreement, the relevant employment regulations or an employment contract. Holidays and non-working days established by law and any period of temporary inability to work confirmed by an authorized physician are not included in the duration of annual leave. Employees may not waive their right to annual leave or accept payment in lieu of annual leave. Any such agreements are null and void. An employee who is employed for the first time or who has been out of work longer than eight days between two consecutive employments is entitled to annual leave after six months of uninterrupted service. Article 78 of the Labour Act regulates the right to proportionate use of annual leave: an employee is entitled to one-twelfth of annual leave for each full month of work in the following cases: if, in the calendar year in which their employment commenced, they did not acquire the right to annual leave because the six-month time limit did not expire; if their employment terminates before the expiration of the six-month time limit. While on annual leave, the employees are entitled to salary compensation, whose amount is set by a collective agreement, the employment regulations or their employment contracts. The salary compensation may not be lower than the employee's average monthly salary in the preceding three months (taking into account any other monetary or in-kind benefits, which represent remuneration for their work). When an employment contract is terminated, the employer is obliged to pay compensation to the employee who has not used their annual leave in full in lieu of their using the annual leave accrued. The compensation is determined in proportion to the number of days of unused annual leave.

An employee has the right to take annual leave in two parts unless otherwise agreed with the employer. If the employee takes annual leave in parts, they must use the first part, lasting at least two weeks without breaks, in the same calendar year in which the annual leave is accrued, provided that the employee has accrued no less than two weeks of annual leave. Any outstanding annual leave may be carried over and must be used no later than 30 June of the next year. The second part of annual leave may not be carried over to the next calendar year, provided that the employer has made it possible for the employee to use this annual leave in the year for which it was acquired. Namely, the rule is to use the right to annual leave in the year for which it was acquired, but the legislator also provides exceptions to that rule. However, if the employee had to interrupt or could not take the whole annual leave or portion thereof in the calendar year in which it was accrued due to illness or maternity, parental or adoption leave, or the leave for having to take care of a child with serious developmental disabilities, they may use it by 30 June of the following year. In case they were not in a position to use or were not allowed by the employer to use it by 30 June of the following calendar year, they are entitled to use it by the end of the calendar year in which they returned to work. A seafarer, an employee working abroad or an employee on duty in national defence forces may take annual leave in its entirety in the following calendar year. The employer will prepare the annual leave schedule in accordance with a collective agreement, the employment regulations, an employment contract and the Labour Act not later than 30 June of the current year and will notify the employees about the schedule. When an employee works part-time for two or more employers, and if the employers fail to reach an agreement about the simultaneous use of annual leave, they must allow the employee to use annual leave in accordance with their wishes. When preparing the annual leave schedule, the employer must take into account the work organization demands and the rest options available to employees. An employee must be notified about the duration and schedule of annual leave at least fifteen days before the annual leave is to be taken. Employees have the right to take one day of annual leave whenever they wish, provided that they notify the employer thereof at least three days in advance unless in cases in which it is not possible for specific justified reasons on the employer's part.

§6. Breaks, Daily Rest, Paid and Unpaid Leave

78. An employee who works at least six hours a day has the right to a paid rest period (a break) of at least thirty minutes each working day unless otherwise specified by a separate law. A minor who works at least four and a half hours a day has the right to a paid rest period (a break) of at least thirty continuous minutes every day. The rest period counts as the working hours. Counting breaks as working time engenders increased costs for employers. If work cannot be interrupted for the purpose of taking a rest period because of its nature, the time and manner of taking rest periods must be regulated by a collective agreement, an agreement between the works council and the employer or an employment contract (Article 73(1–5) Labour Act).

79. According to Article 74 of the Labour Act, in the course of each twenty-four-hour period, an employee is entitled to a daily rest of at least twelve consecutive hours. However, an adult employee performing a seasonal job that involves two periods of work split up over the day is entitled to a daily rest of at least eight consecutive hours if this employee is given an alternative daily rest period equivalent in length to the missed rest hours right after their working time with no rest, or with a shorter period of rest.

80. According to Article 86 of the Labour Act, during the calendar year, an employee has the right to be free from work obligations and to receive salary compensation (paid leave) for important personal reasons, in particular, those related to marriage, childbirth, serious illness or death of a member of the immediate family. The total duration of paid leave may not exceed seven working days a year unless otherwise stipulated in a collective agreement, the employment regulations or an employment contract. The employee is also entitled to paid leave for the purpose of education or vocational training, as well as for education required by the employee's involvement in the works council or trade union. The conditions, duration and remuneration are determined by a collective agreement, an agreement between the works council and the employer or the employment regulations. For the purpose of the acquisition of employment entitlements or other rights related to employment, the periods of paid leave are considered time spent at work. Employees who are voluntary blood donors are entitled to one day off work on the day of blood donation unless otherwise provided for by a collective agreement, an agreement between the works council and the employer or an employment contract.

81. According to Article 87 of the Labour Act, the employer may grant the employee unpaid leave at his or her request. During unpaid leave, the rights and obligations arising from employment or related to employment are suspended unless otherwise specified by the law. During unpaid leave, employees may pay their pension contributions in order not to have breaks in service, which might affect their right to the old-age pension. The employee has the right to unpaid leave for a total of five working days per year to provide personal care to a member of the immediate family or a person living in the same household who needs it due to serious health reasons. Although this leave is unpaid, the employer is obliged to pay social security contributions for his/her employee when the employee is taking this leave.

§7. Maternity: Parental Leave – Breastfeeding Breaks

82. The Maternity and Parental Benefits Act of 2022 regulates the following rights: (1) maternity leave; (2) paternity leave; (3) parental leave; (4) half-time work; (5) half-time work for intensive childcare; (6) breastfeeding breaks; (7) leave for a pregnant employee or an employee who is breastfeeding; (8) day off for a prenatal medical examination; (9) leave or half-time work for the purpose of caring for or nursing a child with severe developmental problems; and (10) suspension of the employment relationship until the child turns three years of age. Maternity leave consists of compulsory and additional maternity leave. It starts twenty-eight days before childbirth and lasts until the child is six months old. A pregnant employee may start using maternity leave earlier in exceptional circumstances: forty-five days before the due date if her medical condition demands it, as confirmed by an authorized physician. The compulsory maternity leave begins twenty-eight days before the due date and lasts for seventy days after childbirth: a total of ninety-eight days. The child's father may start using the additional maternity leave after the completion of the compulsory maternity leave. As already indicated, after the completion of the compulsory maternity leave, either parent may use the additional maternity leave until the child is six months old. The additional maternity leave may be used in the form of half-time work.

83. After the expiry of maternity leave or half-time work, an employed parent has the right to use parental leave. Both parents enjoy this right and can exercise it until the child is eight years old. The right to parental leave should be used by both parents in equal proportion, i.e., four months each or fifteen months each for twins and for the third and every subsequent child. Fathers are encouraged to take parental leave because if the parental leave is used by only one parent (in practice, used mostly by mothers), it is used for a period of six months (instead of eight months, which is the total duration of parental leave when used by both parents) for the first and second-born child, or thirty months for twins, the third and every subsequent child. A parent may use parental leave at once or in parts. If a parent uses parental leave in parts, they may use it not more than twice per year for at least thirty days per segment. Although the legislator envisages that both parents should use parental leave in equal parts, it is a partly transferable right, i.e., only one of the parents may use parental leave if both parents confirm this in writing. Two months are not transferable. In that case, it is used for the duration of six months for the first and second child or twenty-eight months for twins, the third and each subsequent child.

84. In the Annual Report for 2023, the Ombudsperson for Gender Equality continued to warn about the unsustainably low level of use of parental leave by fathers in Croatia. The Ombudsperson published the data of the Croatian Health Insurance Institute (HZZO) concerning maternity and paternal leave users in 2023. The data were used to establish the gender structure of the maternity and paternal leave users, as follows:

- after the expiry of the compulsory maternity leave, 68,246 mothers continued using the leave, compared to only 156 fathers (0.23%);
- paternal leave was used by 46,166 mothers and 2,022 fathers (4.2%).

The data clearly show that an exceedingly low percentage of fathers have used maternity and paternal leave. These data show that much needs to be done in order to achieve equality in parental care. Apart from the traditional gender roles, another reason why fathers do not use maternity and paternal leave may lie in the fact that women, as a rule, work for lower wages.

85. An employee nursing her child is entitled to a breastfeeding break of two hours per day if she is working full-time, regardless of whether the father, who is employed or self-employed, is exercising any of the rights stipulated in the Maternity and Paternal Benefits Act at the same time and for the same child. That right may be exercised once a day for two hours or two times a day for one hour per break, until the child's first birthday. The breastfeeding break counts as working time. An employed mother taking a breastfeeding break is entitled to salary compensation paid by the HZZO. The requirements and the procedure for the exercise of the right to a breastfeeding break are stipulated in greater detail in the 2011 Regulation (Official Gazette Nos. 112/2011 and 152/2022).

Chapter 4. Remuneration

§1. The Notion of Remuneration

86. Although the legislator has defined salary in the Labour Act as an amount of money (an exception here is the way in which the issue of salary is regulated in the context of equal pay for women and men; for more details, *see* paragraphs 93 and 94), some special laws include payments in kind as salary. Thus, for instance, the Income Tax Act of 2016 (last amended in 2023) treats any payments employees receive in kind as equal to payments in money for tax purposes. Receipts in kind are, for instance, the use of buildings, means of transport, more favourable interest rates when approving loans, etc. Under the Labour Act, an employee is entitled to receive salary for the work performed, compensation for work during holidays and Sundays, for night work, for overtime work, for hardship and special conditions and salary compensation for the periods while they have not worked for a justifiable reason.

§2. The Regulation of Remuneration

87. The Labour Act defines the general rules for the determination of the right to salary; the actual amount of money (pay) is determined in other legal sources: special laws (this is the case in the public sector – the Act on Salaries in Civil Service and Public Services of 2023), the employment contracts, employment regulations or collective agreements. Salaries may be determined by an agreement between the works council and the employer (works agreement) only if the trade unions have duly authorized the works council to determine salaries. An employer bound by a collective agreement must not calculate and pay an employee remuneration amounting to less than the amount established by the collective agreement. If the basis and criteria for salaries have not been established by a collective agreement, an employer employing at least twenty employees must establish them in the employment regulations (*see* paragraph 28). If the salary has not been established in this manner and if the employment contract does not contain sufficient data on the basis of which it can be established, the employer is obliged to pay the employee an appropriate salary. An appropriate salary is a salary regularly paid for equal work, and if it is impossible to establish such a salary, then a salary is established by the court, which has taken into account all the circumstances. Salary is paid after the work has been performed. It must be paid in money at intervals not longer than one month. Salary, salary compensation and other receipts are paid within the deadlines set by the collective agreement or employment contract and no later than the fifteenth day of the current month for the previous month. When paying salary, salary compensation or severance pay, the employer must provide an account to the employee from which it is evident how salary, salary compensation or severance pay have been calculated. The employer who fails to pay salary, salary compensation or severance pay on their maturity dates or who fails to pay the full amount must provide the employee with a payroll account for the amount receivable by the end of the month in which the salary, salary compensation or severance pay are due. The payroll accounts are valid as writs of execution.

88. An employee is entitled to a higher salary for arduous working conditions, overtime and night work, and if they have to work on Sundays, holidays, and other days that are not working days according to the law. An employee is entitled to salary compensation for periods in which they have not worked with just cause established by the law, other regulations or a collective agreement.

89. The employer must not, without the consent of the employee, settle their claim against the employee by withholding the payment of salary or part of salary or by withholding the payment of salary compensation or part of salary compensation. An employee may not give consent to such actions in advance before the claim arises.

90. The protection of salary if it is withheld without consent is regulated by the Execution Act of 2012 (last amended in 2024). If salary is subject to execution, the amount equal to two-thirds of the average net salary in Croatia is protected from execution; if the purpose of execution is to collect money for alimony and in other cases defined by law, the protected amount is half of the average net salary in Croatia. An exception is an execution for the purpose of collecting child support, in which case the protected amount is one-fourth of the average net salary paid to the persons employed in the legal entities in Croatia in the previous year. If the debtor receives a salary that is lower than the average net salary in Croatia, the amount protected from execution is two-thirds of the debtor's total salary; if the purpose of execution is to collect alimony, and in other cases defined by law, the protected amount is half of the debtor's net salary.

91. The minimum wage is defined by the Minimum Wage Act of 2018 as amended in 2021. The minimum wage is set once a year, no later than 31 October of the current year. It is determined by a decree of the Government of Croatia at the proposal of the Minister of Labour. It cannot be determined in an amount less than the amount determined for the previous year. When the Minister of Labour makes a proposal on the amount of minimum wage, he needs to bear in mind the increase in the share of the minimum wage in the average gross salary and needs to take into account inflation, salary developments, unemployment and employment trends, demographic trends and the overall state of the economy. Apart from this, the Minister of Labour needs to pay special attention to activities with low salaries and with vulnerable groups of employees and needs to consult with social partners. The minimum wage set by this Act is defined as the lowest monthly gross wage payable to an employee working full-time. It currently amounts to EUR 840 gross. Exceptionally, the minimum wage is considered to be the lowest monthly gross wage according to the complexity of the work for full-time work, agreed by the collective agreement, the application of which has been extended by the ministerial decree. The average net salary paid to the employees in the legal entities in Croatia in 2023 was EUR 1,148. The average gross salary paid to the employees in the legal entities in Croatia in 2023 was EUR 1,584.

§3. EQUAL PAY

92. According to ILO Convention No. 100 ratified by Croatia and the Labour Act of 2014 (last amended in 2023), an employer must pay equal salaries to women and men for equal work and for work of equal value. Furthermore, the Labour Act provides that two persons of different genders are considered to be performing equal work and work of equal value if:

– they perform the same work in the same or similar conditions or if they could substitute one another at the workplace;
– the work one of them performs is of a similar nature to that performed by the other, and the differences between the work performed by them and the conditions under which it is performed do not affect the overall nature of the work, or they appear so rarely that they do not affect the overall nature of the work.

Work of equal value is performed by two persons of different genders if the work performed by one of them is of equal value to the work performed by the other, taking into account the qualification obtained at a certain level of education and the nature of the work determined according to objective criteria such as required knowledge, skills, responsibility and independence and the conditions in which the work is performed.

In order to exercise the right to equal pay for women and men, the employer is obliged, at the request of the employee, to provide the employee with information on the criteria on the basis of which the employee who performs tasks of the same or similar nature received the salary, if such an employee exists.

93. There have been a few studies aimed at shedding light on the issue of the gender wage gap in Croatia. Nestić (2007)[1] and a study conducted by the Ombudsman for Gender Equality (2010) found that only a more equitable sharing of family responsibilities between parents, including the use of parental leave, could significantly reduce the part of the gap that is due to child-related absence from work. Furthermore, the study conducted by the Ombudsman for Gender Equality showed that the main reason for the gap is the gender-based perception of different jobs as being more appropriate for persons of one or the other gender. This perception results in gender segregation in the labour market: jobs where men have the dominant share achieve a higher price on the market. The more recent study ('Bridging the Gender Pay Gap in the Western Balkans', 2024) found the widest gap in the financial and insurance sector, health sector, social work activities and manufacturing industry. The gender pay gap in Croatia stands at 7.4% (2022) and it represents a decrease compared to 13.3% (2018), but the study indicates that the gender pay gap decrease was a spontaneous process that could not be attributed to planned policies or measures.

1. D. Nestić, *Differing Characteristics or Differing Rewards: What Is Behind the Gender Wage Gap in Croatia?* (Zagreb 2007).

§4. REMUNERATION IN CASE OF TEMPORARY NON-PERFORMANCE OF WORK

I. Sickness

94. The Mandatory Health Insurance Act of 2013 (last amended in 2023) provides that employees are entitled to salary compensation during sick leave. For the first forty-two days of sick leave, this salary compensation is paid by the employer and thereafter by the Health Insurance Institute, which uses the funds from the State Budget. The salary compensation base is the average salary paid to the employee (insured person) in the last six months. In order to be entitled to the full amount of the salary compensation during sick leave, an employee must be insured for a certain time (employment of at least nine months without breaks or twelve months with breaks over the past two years). Persons who do not meet the requirement of previous insurance status are entitled to reduced salary compensation (25% of the salary compensation base). Salary compensation may not be lower than 70% of the salary compensation base. The lowest monthly salary compensation for employees working full-time is 25% of the base used for the calculation, i.e., EUR 110.36. The highest monthly salary compensation for employees working full-time, when paid from the HZZO funds, is the salary compensation base increased by 28%, i.e., EUR 565.04. The legislator envisages cases when salary compensation is paid directly by the HZZO from the day an employee becomes temporarily unable to work. This is done when the insured person must be kept in isolation because they carry a disease or because there has been an outbreak of a contagious disease in their midst; when living tissue and organs are to be transplanted to another person insured by the HZZO; when an employee has an illness or complications related to pregnancy or childbirth; when an employee is using maternity leave or is using their right to work half-time; when an employee has taken compassionate leave for the death of a child, stillbirth or death of a child during maternity leave; when an employee is unable to work because of a wound, injury or illness that has been directly caused by their participation in the Homeland War. According to the Mandatory Health Insurance Act, the insured (the employee) is not entitled to salary compensation if: (1) they deliberately caused the temporary work incapacity; (2) they failed to notify the appointed primary-care physician of their illness within three days of the onset of illness, i.e., within three days of the cessation of the circumstances that had prevented them from notifying the physician; (3) they deliberately prevented their recovery or the restoration of their work capacity; (4) they worked in the course of sick leave; (5) they failed, without just cause, to respond to an invitation to undergo a medical examination; (6) they did not follow the treatment instructions, or if they left the place of domicile without the consent of the appointed primary-care physical or abused the right to sick leave in some other manner.

II. Pregnancy and Maternity

95. The Maternity and Parental Benefits Act of 2022 stipulates the manner in which salary compensation is to be calculated in nine of the ten cases provided by the Act. The ten rights are: maternity leave, paternity leave, parental leave, half-time work, half-time work for intensified childcare, breastfeeding break, leave for a pregnant employee or an employee who is breastfeeding, a day off for a prenatal check-up, leave or half-time work for the purpose of caring for or nursing a child with severe developmental problems and the right to suspension of the employment until the child's third birthday. No salary compensation is receivable while a person is exercising the right to the suspension of employment until the child's third birthday. As for who pays the compensation and the actual amount, this depends on the right in question (*see* more details in the next paragraph). In some cases, it is set at 100%, in other cases at 70%, and in some cases at 50% of the salary compensation base.

96. While an employed or self-employed parent is using the right to maternity leave, the right to additional maternity leave in the form of half-time work, the right to parental leave, the right to breastfeeding break, as well as in the case when the child dies during the maternity or parental leave (three months from the date of the child's death), the parents are entitled to salary compensation to the amount of 100% of the salary compensation base determined in line with the regulations concerning mandatory health insurance. The base for the determination of the salary compensation for a person in employment is the average salary in the last six months before the month in which this person started exercising his right. Salary compensation may not be lower than EUR 309 – 70% of the salary compensation base set by the Act on the Execution of the State Budget of the Republic of Croatia of 2024 at EUR 441.44. No maximum amount has been set for salary compensation during maternity leave and additional maternity leave is used in the form of half-time work. However, salary compensation during parental leave is calculated in the same way as salary compensation during maternity leave, but there is a cap: it may not exceed 225.5% of the base (it may not exceed EUR 995.45). After the birth of a child, a working father is entitled to paid paternity leave for an uninterrupted period, depending on the number of children born: ten working days for one child; fifteen working days in case of birth of twins, triplets or simultaneous birth of several children. It can be taken until the child is six months old.

97. Salary compensation for maternity leave and additional maternity leave used in the form of half-time work is paid from the HZZO funds; salary compensation for all other rights guaranteed by the Act on Maternity and Parental Benefits is paid from the state budget. There is a single exception. Namely, if an employee who is pregnant, has given birth or is breastfeeding works in a job that is detrimental to her health or to the health of the child she is nursing, she is entitled to salary compensation to the amount of the average salary paid in the last three months before the month in which she becomes entitled to this leave. Salary compensation is paid by the employer. In the period in which an employed or self-employed parent exercises the right to maternity leave, paternal leave, half-time work, compassionate leave for the death of a child, breastfeeding break, leave that may be used by a pregnant employee, an employee who has given birth or is breastfeeding and the rights pertaining to an employed or self-employed parent of a child with serious developmental problems, such employed or self-employed parents are entitled to all the rights related to the mandatory pension insurance and to the right to contributions under special regulations. The rights of an employed parent stipulated by the Maternity and Parental Benefits Act of 2022 may be made more extensive in a collective agreement, an agreement between the works council and the employer, the employment regulations and an employment contract, at the expense of the employer, under the conditions and in the manner defined in the relevant act of the employer.

Chapter 5. Employee Liability

98. If an employee suffers damage at work or in relation to work, the employer must compensate the employee for the damage according to the general provisions of the Civil Obligations Act of 2005 (amended in 2023), Articles 1045 through 1072. The employer is liable for all degrees of culpability (simple negligence, gross negligence and intent). In order for the employer to be held liable, there must be a causal relationship between harmful action and damage. When there is no causal relationship between the work process and the control thereof and the actual injury sustained by the employee, the employer is not liable for the damage caused to the employee (VSRH, Revr-662/08 of 4 February 2009). Even when there is strict liability for the damage, there must be a causal relationship between the harmful action and the damage. If there is no such relationship, there is no liability for the damage (VSRH, Rev-1306/06 of 28 February 2007). Strict (objective) liability is stipulated generally for all damage caused by objects or activities with a higher risk to the environment; it is up to the court to decide on a case-to-case basis whether the object or the activity with a higher risk for the environment related to the damage is indeed an object or an activity with a higher risk for the environment (Constitutional Court, U-III-1062/2005). Furthermore, the Health and Safety Act of 2014 (last amended in 2018) envisages in Article 25 strict liability of the employer if the damage suffered by the employee was caused by an injury sustained at work, an occupational disease or a work-related disease. An employer may only be held safe from this liability, or the liability may be limited if the events occurred due to exceptional and unforeseeable circumstances, i.e., due to force majeure, or intent or gross negligence of the employee or a third party, or if the employer was unable to influence the course of events despite exercising the measures of occupational health and safety. The jurisprudence of the VSRH has cases in which the employers were held safe from liability for the damage. Thus, for instance, when there are no omissions on the part of the employer in the organization and health and safety system, the employer will not be liable for the damage suffered by an employee as a consequence of an illness (death caused by stroke), despite the fact that the illness occurred while the employee was on a business trip (VSRH, Rev-2401/98 of 26 January 2000). The right to compensation for the damage is also obtained if the damage is caused by the employer to the employee by a violation of the employee's rights arising from employment.

99. Article 1061 of the Civil Obligations Act deals with the liability of the employer for the damage caused by an employee either at work or related to work to a third party. The employer who employs the employee at the time when the damage was caused is liable for the damage unless the employer is able to prove the existence of reasons which hold the employee safe. The injured party is entitled to seek redress for the damage from the employee directly if the damage was caused with intent. The employer who compensated the injured party for the damage caused is entitled to seek compensation for the costs incurred in the redress of the damage from the employee if the employee has caused the damage intentionally or due to gross negligence. This right of the employer expires six months after the day when the damage was redressed. The Labour Act (Articles 107 and 110) also envisages the liability of an employee to refund compensation for the damage ('recourse liability'). If an employee causes damage to a third party at the workplace or in relation to the work, either intentionally or due to gross negligence, and compensation for the damage has been paid by the employer, the employer can claim from the employee the amount of compensation paid to the third party. Collective agreements or employment regulations may establish the conditions and methods for reducing compensation for the damage or exempting an employee from the obligation to pay compensation for the damage.

100. The Labour Act in Articles 107 through 110 contains more favourable provisions for the employee's liability for the damage caused to the employer. While the employer is liable for all degrees of culpability, the employee is not liable for damage caused by simple negligence. An employee who, at the workplace or in relation to the work, either intentionally or due to gross negligence, causes the employer to suffer damage must compensate the employer for such damage. If the damage has been caused by several employees, each employee is liable for part of the damage caused by them. If it is impossible to determine which part of the damage was caused by which employee, all the employees are considered to be equally liable and must compensate for the damage in equal parts. If several employees have caused damage by a premeditated criminal offence, they are jointly liable for the damage caused.

101. The jurisprudence has clearly defined the concept of an accident at work. As stated by the VSRH, an accident at work is an accident suffered by an employee not only in the performance of their job based on the employment contract but also in the performance of other tasks at the demand and for the benefit of the employer during working hours and inside the employer's premises. The employer is liable for this damage (VSRH, Revr-319/07 of 30 September 2008). However, according to the Supreme Court's jurisprudence, the damage caused outside of the work process suffered by the plaintiff in a traffic accident that occurred as the plaintiff was driving home from work is neither damage caused in the workplace nor damage related to work. As there is no causal relationship between the occurrence of the damage and the tasks performed by the employee for the employer in line with the employment contract, the employer is not liable for the damage (VSRH, Revt 133/07 of 29 April 2008).

102. A predetermined amount of compensation for the damage could be stipulated in a collective agreement or employment regulations only if determining the actual damage would cause disproportionate costs. In that case, the amount of compensation for damages for certain harmful acts may be determined in advance. The harmful acts and compensation may be provided for in the collective agreement or employment regulations. If the damage caused by a harmful act is much greater than the predetermined compensation, the employer may claim compensation for the amount of the damage actually suffered and established. As determined by jurisprudence, the employer is not authorized to withhold the compensation unilaterally from the employee's salary (VSRH, Rev-2322/98 of 13 March 2002).

103. The Labour Act (Article 51) contains a provision on the compensation for the damage caused in the course of the work performed by a temporary agency worker in the user undertaking. The damage caused by a temporary agency worker at the workplace or in relation to work in the user undertaking to a third party must be compensated by the user undertaking, which may claim the compensation for the costs incurred in the redress of the damage from the temporary agency worker if such damage was caused by the temporary agency worker intentionally or due to gross negligence. The temporary work agency is liable for the damage caused to the user undertaking by a temporary agency worker at the workplace or in relation to work according to the Civil Obligations Act. If a temporary agency worker suffers damage at the workplace or in relation to work for the user undertaking, they may claim compensation from the temporary work agency or the user undertaking.

Chapter 6. Termination of Employment Contract

104. A contract of employment is terminated, according to Article 112(1) of the Labour Act:

1. upon the death of the employee;
2. upon the death of employer-natural person;
3. upon the death of employer-sole trader, if in accordance with the separate law, the small business was not transferred;
4. termination of small business by virtue of law in accordance with a separate law;
5. upon the expiration of the period for which a fixed-term employment contract has been concluded;
6. when the employee has turned 65 years of age and has accrued fifteen years of employment service unless otherwise agreed by the employer and the employee;
7. by means of an agreement between the employer and the employee;
8. upon the submission of a legally effective decision on retirement due to permanent incapacity to work;
9. by dismissal;
10. by a decision of the competent court.

This provision contains an exhaustive list (*numerus clausus*) of the ways in which an employment contract may be terminated.

§1. The Death of the Employee or Employer; Termination of Small Business

105. Personal performance of work is a substantial element of the employment relationship. The employment relationship is relationship *intuitu personae*. Because of the nature of this relationship, the Labour Act has explicitly stipulated that the employment contract is terminated by the death of the employee and by the death of the employer-natural person. For instance, if the employee was a nurse, a private tutor or a private secretary of the employer, the employer's death terminates the employment contract. Furthermore, when the erstwhile employer's successors do not take over the running of a small business, it is a reason for the termination of small business by virtue of law, and consequently, the employment contracts of the employees will be terminated.

§2. Expiry of the Fixed-Time Contract

106. Croatian legislation has set certain restrictions on the conclusion of fixed-term contracts. When the parties sign such contracts, the employer needs to provide a justifiable reason why this type of contract is offered.. Furthermore, it can be concluded for a maximum duration of three years and the employer must not conclude more than three consecutive fixed-term employment contracts with the same employee for a continuous period exceeding three years, except in order to substitute a temporarily absent employee or where it is on objective grounds allowed by the law or a collective agreement. If a fixed-term employment contract was concluded contrary to the provisions of the Labour Act or if the employee continued working for the employer after the expiration of the period for which the contract had originally been made, the employee is considered to have concluded an open-ended employment contract.

§3. Retirement

107. According to the Labour Act (Article 112(6)), a contract of employment is terminated when the employee has turned 65 years of age and has accrued fifteen years of service unless otherwise agreed by the employer and the employee. The practice in Croatia has been for the employees whose employment contract is terminated because they have met the pension requirements to receive severance pay determined by the relevant collective agreement (usually four average monthly salaries). Thus, as soon as an employee becomes eligible for retirement (the requirements listed above are the requirements for an old-age pension envisaged in Article 33 of the Pension Insurance Act), the employer has the right to issue a declaratory decision on the termination of the employment contract and is not compelled to comply with the provisions on the dismissal of the employment contract (*inter alia*, there is no obligation to comply with the notice period; under the law, there is no severance pay entitlement). This is an exception to the general prohibition of age discrimination; in light of ever-increasing life expectancy and medical advances that have made our lives longer, healthier and more active, a decision should be made whether to retain this derogation from the prohibition of the non-discrimination principle. The Croatian Act on Higher Education and Scientific Activity of 2022 (51) envisages that employees employed in teaching positions in higher education institutions shall have their employment contracts terminated at the end of the calendar year in which they turn 65 for the purpose of retirement. Exceptionally, with a tenured full professor, a tenured scientific advisor and a tenured professor of professional studies, a public higher education institution or a public scientific institute, at the expense of its own funds, can enter into an employment contract at the latest until the end of the academic or calendar year in which s/he turned seventy years of life. Furthermore, the Croatian Civil Servants Act of 2023 (amended in 2024), Article 152(1)(3), envisages that civil servants face compulsory retirement from civil service when they turn 65 and when they have at least fifteen years of service unless the head of the civil service body and the civil servant agree otherwise, taking into account the needs of the service. In addition to the legislation quoted above, there are some special pieces of legislation in force in Croatia; their stipulations on age as the reason for the termination of the employment contract or service differ from those in the Labour Act. The Croatian Constitution contains a provision in Article 120(2) stipulating that the age of 70 constitutes grounds for compulsory dismissal of judges from judicial office. As regards employees employed in particularly difficult jobs that are harmful to their health and ability to work or employees whose physiological functions of the organism decline after a certain age due to the nature and severity of the work to such an extent that they prevent the further successful performance of that work, the relevant provisions are contained in the Act on Accelerated Pension Insurance Periods of 2018 (amended in 2021). For instance, some jobs, such as professional fishermen and jobs in road traffic (drivers of trams and buses in public transport), have accelerated pension plans. Jobs of pilots, ballet dancers, opera singers, etc., have accelerated pension plans as well; the pensionable age for these posts is lower (Article 27 of the Act on Accelerated Pension Insurance Periods).

§4. Termination by Mutual Consent

108. According to the principle of freedom of contract, it is always possible to terminate the employment contract by mutual consent. Unlike dismissal, which is a unilateral legal act, the agreement on the termination of the employment contract is a bilateral legal act, although it may be contained in two separate written statements, one offering and the other accepting the offer to sign such an agreement. The termination agreement can be concluded without any legal restrictions, but it must be in writing in order to be legally valid (Article 113 of the Labour Act). The date of the termination of the employment contract is agreed upon by the parties. The provisions of the Labour Act regarding dismissal do not apply; consequently, the employee is not entitled to severance pay, but the parties may agree on it. For instance, when an employment contract is terminated by mutual consent because the employee is retiring, the employee is, as a rule, entitled to severance pay based on a collective agreement, employment regulations, the employment contract or the agreement to terminate an employment contract.

§5. General Work Incapacity

109. According to Article 112(8) of the Labour Act, an employment contract is terminated upon submission of a legally effective decision on the recognition of the right to disability pension due to permanent work incapacity. As this is not dismissal but a special type of termination of an employment contract, the employee is not entitled under the law to a notice period and severance pay. The decision of the employer to terminate the employment contract is of a declarative nature in this case. If an employee meets the criteria for the disability pension due to occupational work incapacity, the employment contract will not be terminated: under Article 41 of the Labour Act, the employer will be obliged to offer the employee another job and to adapt to the workplace and the working conditions to the employee's ability (reasonable accommodation). If there are no appropriate jobs, the employer may dismiss the employee with a disability only with the approval of the works council and is obliged to pay double severance pay (for more details, *see* paragraph 41).

§6. Judicial Termination of the Contract

110. Article 125 of the Labour Act authorizes the court to dissolve an employment contract by issuing a decision to that effect, if petitioned to do so by the employer or the employee in cases of unlawful dismissal. The judicial termination of the employment contract is predicated on unlawful dismissal. If an employee has been unlawfully dismissed, they are entitled to be reinstated in the same job they had been doing previously. However, according to the Labour Act, both the employer and the employee may file a request for the judicial termination of the employment contract until the conclusion of the trial before the Court of First Instance. The language of the provision is somewhat baffling, given that the parties to an employment contract file a request for the judicial termination of the employment contract before the court has ruled on the permissibility of the dismissal. The case law is for the employees to challenge the lawfulness of their dismissal by filing a legal suit and for the employer to file a counter-suit petitioning the court to issue a decision on the judicial dissolution of the contract. The court will dissolve the employment contract at the request of the employee if the employee does not find it acceptable to continue working for the employer. The requirements that must be met by the employer who files for judicial dissolution of an employment contract are more stringent than for an employee. An employee must state that it is not acceptable for them to continue employment. In order for an employment contract to be judicially dissolved at the request of an employer, the court must find that it is impossible for the employment to continue ('if circumstances exist which reasonably demonstrate that, in view of all the circumstances and interests of both contracting parties, the continuation of employment is not possible', Article 125(2) of the Labour Act). When the court establishes that a dismissal by an employer is not permissible (not in accordance with the provisions of the Labour Act) and that it is not acceptable for the employee to continue employment, the court, upon the employee's request, determines the date of the termination of employment and awards them damages in an amount not less than three and not more than eight monthly salaries, depending on the length of employment, age and maintenance obligations lying upon the employee (e.g., support of dependent family members).

§7. Dismissal

I. Extraordinary Dismissal

111. According to Article 116 of the Labour Act, employers and employees may invoke just cause and cancel an open-ended or fixed-term employment contract, without having to comply with a prescribed or agreed notice period if, due to an extremely grave violation of an employment obligation or due to any other highly relevant fact and recognizing all the circumstances or interests of both contracting parties, it is not possible to continue employment. An employment contract may be terminated by extraordinary dismissal not later than fifteen days after the day when the person concerned learned about the fact that led to the extraordinary dismissal. Prior to extraordinary dismissal (and indeed, to ordinary dismissal) due to the employee's conduct or performance, the employer must give the employee an opportunity to present the defence unless, due to circumstances, the employer cannot be reasonably expected to do so (Article 119(2) of the Labour Act).

112. The most common cause of extraordinary dismissal is a gross violation of the obligations arising from employment on the part of the employee. The following reasons have been accepted as just cause for extraordinary dismissal in the Croatian case law: unsatisfactory work results; the employee's conflict with the employer; defaming and insulting the employer; the employee's conflicts with other employees; unjustified refusal to perform tasks; when the employee is in custody; criminal offences or misdemeanours committed by the employee; theft of the employer's property; private engagements during working hours; unjustified absence from work or unjustified desertion of the workplace; violation of the prohibition of competition with the employer; participation in an illegal strike action; loss of a special permit or licence to perform a job. However, the Croatian courts have found that there are no legally valid reasons for extraordinary dismissal if the employer introduces changes to the work organization because this is deemed to be a business risk to be borne by the employer. According to the case law of the VSRH, if a criminal report is filed against the employee, this fact in and of itself is not deemed to be an especially relevant fact that constitutes a valid reason for a dismissal. In most cases, employees resort to an extraordinary termination of their employment contracts when their salaries have not been paid for several months.

113. A party to an employment contract that terminates the contract by giving extraordinary notice is entitled to claim compensation for the damage caused by the non-performance of the obligations from the employment contract from the party who is responsible for the dismissal (Article 116(3) of the Labour Act).

114. Article 35 of the Labour Act allows an employee exercising rights related to the protection of parenthood (such as maternity leave, parental leave, etc.) and a pregnant employee to terminate their employment contract by extraordinary dismissal.

115. The works council plays an important role in the extraordinary dismissal procedure: if the works council opposes an extraordinary dismissal and the employee files a legal suit to challenge the permissibility of the dismissal, demanding from the employer to be reinstated, the employer must reinstate the employee to their job within eight days of the service of the dismissal notice and of the proof of the initiation of the legal suit and retain them in employment pending a final judicial decision on the merits (Article 150(9) of the Labour Act). If the employer terminates the employment contract by extraordinary dismissal due to an extremely grave violation of an employment obligation on the part of the employee, the employer may suspend the employee pending a final judicial decision on the permissibility of the dismissal. In this case, the employer must pay the employee monthly salary compensation equal to half of the average salary paid to the employee in the preceding three months (Article 150(10) of the Labour Act). If the works council's opposition to an extraordinary dismissal is manifestly unfounded or is in contravention of the provisions of the Labour Act, the employer may move the court to issue an interim measure releasing them from the obligation to return the employee to work and to pay the employee salary compensation, pending a final judicial decision on the merits (Article 150(11) of the Labour Act).

II. Ordinary Dismissal

116. Both the ordinary and extraordinary termination of the employment contract constitute a unilateral expression of the will of either the employee or the employer to terminate the employment contract. Ordinary dismissal differs from extraordinary dismissal in that the former requires the terminating party to honour the notice period. This obligation does not obtain in the case of extraordinary dismissal. In order to protect the weaker contracting party, i.e., the employee, the legislator has devoted particular attention in the Labour Act to the regulation of the issue of the termination of the employment contract by the employer. While the employee may terminate the employment contract without stating the cause, the employer must show cause when terminating the contract. Justifiable causes are listed in the Labour Act. In any case, the dismissal must be submitted in writing.

A. *Just Causes*

117. Article 115 of the Labour Act lists four legitimate reasons that justify ordinary dismissal of an employee by an employer: (1) if the job is no longer necessary due to economic, technological or organizational reasons (dismissal due to business reasons); (2) if the employee is not capable of performing their employment-related duties because of some permanent characteristics or abilities (dismissal due to personal reasons); (3) if the employee has violated the obligations arising from employment (dismissal due to the employee's misconduct); and (4) if the employee did not satisfy during the probationary period (dismissal due to incompetence during probationary period). The Croatian courts have rich case law on just and unjust causes for dismissal. According to the case law, in order for the criteria for a dismissal due to business reasons to be met, it is not necessary for a post to be abolished; it is sufficient for the number of employees engaged in a job to be reduced (VSRH, Revr-70/04 of 26 May 2004). Furthermore, the Croatian courts have taken the position that the reduction of the scope of work alone, rather than the concomitant failure of the expectations that there would be an increase in the amount of business, constitutes a just cause for dismissal due to business reasons (VSRH, Revr-407/03 of 20 May 2004). When considering whether dismissal is permissible or not, the Croatian courts, as a rule, refrain from analysing whether the employer's assessment that there is no longer a need for the employee's services is justified or not. Potočnjak (2007) notes that the Croatian courts have rightly reduced their role to checking whether the formal aspects of the permissibility of dismissal have been met (whether all the legal provisions on the dismissal procedure have been complied with) and preventing the employers from abusing their powers in the sphere of the termination of employment contracts. There are concerns that were the courts to intervene more deeply; the judges would end up making employee-related business policy decisions for the companies. This would restrict free enterprise. The Labour Act contains another employment safety mechanism: the employer who has dismissed an employee for economic, technological or organizational reasons must not employ another employee in the same job for the following six months. If, within that time, a need arises for the employment of a person who would perform the same job, the employer is obliged to offer the employment contract to the employee who was dismissed for business reasons. If the employer fails to do that and employs another person, they have committed a misdemeanour.

118. In the case of dismissal due to personal reasons, the reason for the dismissal does not lie with the employer but with the employee. As noted above, in this case, the employee is not capable of fulfilling their employment-related duties because of some permanent characteristics or abilities. Croatian employers resort to this type of dismissal relatively seldom. The Croatian courts have taken the position that the cause for dismissal due to personal reasons exists when an employee fails to achieve results in their job because of their characteristics or abilities (VSRH, Rev-3048/99 of 9 November 2000) and when an employee has lost the licence to perform the relevant job (these circumstances constitute cause for extraordinary dismissal as well) (VSRH, Rev-115/01 of 9 July 2003). As the inability to perform the obligations arising from employment may occur due to an illness, i.e., through no fault of the employee, the Labour Act envisages in this context some restrictions on the right to dismiss an employee. If a temporary inability is the result of work (occupational disease or accident at work), i.e., of risks that must be borne by the employer, the employer may not dismiss the employee for as long as they remain incapacitated. If a temporary inability is not caused by work (non-occupational illness or injury not sustained at work), this is not of itself the cause for dismissal due to personal reasons. However, if a disease (occupational or non-occupational) has resulted in a permanent change of the characteristics and abilities of the employee with a concomitant inability to perform the obligations arising from employment, the employer can legally dismiss this employee.

119. There are ample jurisprudence reasons for a dismissal due to the employee's conduct: responsibility of an employee who worked as a driver for a traffic accident; lateness and absence from work without justification; performing tasks for the benefit of the company owned by the employee and using the employer's assets for this work during working hours; insulting, humiliating and physically assaulting associates; failure to use proper health and safety equipment, etc. However, the courts have found that there are no grounds for a dismissal due to the misconduct by the employee in the following cases: when employees did not work because they were prevented from working by the employer; if the employer has warned the employee about faults in their work but has not made it possible to rectify the faults; an employee cannot be dismissed simply because there has been a till shortage in the shop where the employee works if a causal relationship between the employee's negligence and the till shortage has not been established, etc. In deciding whether to terminate the employment of an employee guilty of misconduct by extraordinary or ordinary dismissal due to misconduct, the employer must consider carefully whether this is an extremely grave violation of an employment obligation or any other highly relevant fact and if recognizing all the circumstances or interests of both contracting parties, a continuation of the employment is not possible, the employer may resort to extraordinary dismissal.

120. In addition to the reasons for dismissal analysed above, the Labour Act envisages the possibility for the employer to terminate the employment contract if an employee has not performed in a satisfactory manner during the probationary period; the employee must be given notice of at least seven days (Article 53). Likewise, if an employee must pass a professional examination at the end of the traineeship or apprenticeship, the employer may dismiss (ordinary dismissal) the trainee or apprentice who has not passed the professional examination (Article 58(3)). Furthermore, a *lex specialis* (Insolvency Act of 2015, amended in 2014) stipulates that instituting bankruptcy proceedings constitutes a valid reason for the termination of an employment contract.

B. *The Guarantee of a Minimum Term of Notice*

121. Unlike extraordinary dismissal, which becomes effective immediately (as soon as a written letter of dismissal is served), with ordinary dismissal, the termination of the contract becomes effective only after the expiry of the notice period. The minimum term of notice is regulated by the Labour Act (Article 122); the term of notice may be regulated in a manner more favourable for the employees in a collective agreement, employment regulations or an employment contract. The Labour Act stipulates that the minimum term of notice depends on the continuous duration of the employment contract, the employee's age, the reason for the termination and the party terminating the contract. Depending on the previous continuous duration of the employment contract, the notice period may last from two weeks (if the employee has been employed with the same employer for less than one year without any breaks in service) up to three months (if the employee has been employed with the same employer for twenty years without any breaks in service). An additional criterion for the determination of the minimum notice period is the employee's age. An employee who has been employed with the same employer for twenty years without any breaks in service will have the notice period extended by two weeks if they are above the age of 50 and one month if they are above the age of 55. Furthermore, as a form of sanction, if the dismissal was caused by the employee's misconduct, the notice period is cut by half. The final element for the determination of the notice period is the party terminating the contract. The legislator favours the employees who terminate their contract by putting in the Labour Act a provision stipulating that when an employment contract is terminated by the employee, the notice period may not exceed one month if the employee has an especially important reason for such notice period. Legal doctrine has been critical of this provision in the Labour Act as insufficiently precise. It is unclear how long the notice period is to last in that case: a month or less, and the content of the phrase 'especially important reason' is just as unclear. In this case, the employee has the burden of proof of the 'especially important reason'.

122. In the course of the notice period, the employee and the employer must perform all their obligations arising from employment. The jurisprudence of the Croatian courts contains a case in which the failure to perform tasks or failure to perform them properly during the notice period resulted in extraordinary dismissal, which was adjudicated to have been justified (VSRH, Rev-1106/01 of 7 October 2003). The employer may, of course, release the employee from the obligation to work during the notice period. If an employee, upon the employer's request, ceases to work before the expiration of the prescribed or agreed notice period, the employer is obliged to pay salary compensation and recognize all the other rights as if the employee had actually worked until the expiry of the notice period (Article 122(4) of the Labour Act).

123. During the notice period, the employee has the right to be absent from work not less than four hours per week with salary compensation for the purpose of seeking new employment. If an employment contract has been terminated by the employee, the collective agreement or employment contract may specify a shorter notice period for the employee than for the employer (Article 122(5–6) of the Labour Act).

124. The notice period starts running on the day of the submission of the notice of dismissal, which must be in writing. The notice period does not run during pregnancy, maternity leave, leave granted to a parent caring for a child with serious developmental problems, exercise of the right to work reduced hours by a parent or adoptive parent, adoption leave, temporary inability to work, annual leave, paid leave, military service, and other types of justifiable absence from work, as prescribed by the Labour Act or by another law (Article 121(3) of the Labour Act).

III. Role of the Works Council in Dismissal Cases

125. In Croatia, the Labour Act grants the employees the right to co-determination through works councils only if they work for the so-called big employers, which have at least twenty employees. Employees in public administration bodies do not enjoy that right. It is important to note that where the works council has not been established, its role is assumed by the shop steward. As the Labour Law precludes the employees working for the so-called small employers (with less than twenty employees) and the employees in the public administration bodies from co-determination, these employees do not enjoy the protection of the works council or the subsidiary protection of their shop steward in the course of the dismissal procedure. Under the Labour Law, the powers of the works council will depend on the actual case: whether the dismissal was ordinary or extraordinary and whether the works council has the right to be consulted or the right of co-decision in the dismissal procedure. As a rule, the employer is obliged to consult the works council before terminating each employment contract. Exceptionally, some categories of employees enjoy special protection from dismissal, and the employer must obtain the consent of the works council prior to dismissing such employees: the works council members, candidates who stood for election for the works council and have not been elected for a period of three months following the election results, employees, who due to an injury at work or an occupational disease have a reduced work capacity with the remaining working capacity or a reduced work capacity with partial loss of work capacity as well as employees with disability, employees over 60 years of age and employee representatives on the supervisory board and board of directors. If the employer fails to comply with their obligations regarding the participation of the works council in the dismissal procedure, the dismissal is null and void.

126. In order for the works council to be able to perform its consultative function, the information related to the proposed dismissal must be forwarded to the works council in its entirety and in due time so that the council may have an opportunity to put forward its comments and proposals in order for the results of the discussion to have a material impact on decision-making. Unless otherwise specified by an agreement between the employer and the works council, the works council must forward its observations about a proposed decision to the employer within eight days. In case of extraordinary dismissal, this deadline is five days (Article 150(5) of the Labour Act). If the works council fails to provide its comments about the proposed decision by this deadline, it is presumed that it does not have any comments and proposals. The works council may oppose dismissal if the employer does not have just cause for it or if the dismissal procedure specified in the Labour Act has not been honoured. The works council must state the reasons for its opposition to the employer's decision. If the works council opposes extraordinary dismissal and the employee files a legal suit to challenge the permissibility of dismissal demanding that the employer reinstate them to their job, the employer must reinstate the employee to work within eight days of the notification about the legal suit and retain them at work pending a final judicial decision on the merits. If the works council's opposition to an extraordinary dismissal is manifestly not founded on the provisions of the Labour Act, the employer may petition the court to issue an interim measure releasing them from the obligation to restore the employee to work and to pay the employee salary compensation pending a final judicial decision on the merits. If the employer terminates an employment contract by extraordinary dismissal due to an extremely grave violation of an employment obligation by the employee, the employer may suspend the employee pending a final judicial decision on the permissibility of dismissal. In this case, the employer must pay the employee a monthly salary compensation equal to half of the average salary paid to the employee in the preceding three months. Any decision rendered by the employer which is contrary to the provisions of the Labour Act governing the consultations with the works council is null and void (Article 150(8 through 12) of the Labour Act).

127. The categories of employees who enjoy special protection against dismissal have already been listed: the works council members, candidates who stood for election for the works council and have not been elected for a period of three months following the election results, employees who due to an injury at work or an occupational disease have a reduced capacity for work as well as employees with disability, employees over 60 years of age and employee representatives on the supervisory board and board of directors. They may not have their employment contracts terminated without the prior consent of the works council (Article 151(1) of the Labour Act). If the works council fails to give or withhold its consent within eight days, its consent is presumed (Article 151(3) of the Labour Act). If the works council refuses to give its consent, the employer may, within fifteen days of the receipt of the statement of the refusal to give consent, ask that such consent be replaced by a judicial decision or an arbitration award (Article 151(4) of the Labour Act). The Court of First Instance must render its decision in the legal action within thirty days of the day of the filing of the action (Article 151(5) of the Labour Act). An agreement between the employer and the works council may also regulate other issues in which the employer may render a decision only subject to the prior consent of the works council (Article 151(6) of the Labour Act).

128. Apart from participating in the decisions on individual terminations of employment contracts, the works council is involved in co-determination in the process of collective redundancies (*see* more in paragraphs 138 and 139). The works council likewise plays a part in the decisions to introduce new technology or changes in the work organization or process because such decisions may result in dismissals.

129. In addition to the part the shop stewards play in the dismissal process when they assume the role of the works council where no such council has been established, the trade unions, under the Labour Act, have the power to participate in the process of deciding on dismissals (*see* more in paragraph 137).

IV. Special Protection for Specific Groups

A. *Pregnancy and Parenthood*

130. According to Article 34(1) of the Labour Act, during pregnancy, maternity and parental leave, the exercise of the right to half-time work by parents or adoptive parents, adoption leave and leave granted to care of a child with serious developmental problems, and in the fifteen days after the cessation of pregnancy or the cessation of the exercise of these rights, the employer may not dismiss from work a pregnant employee or a person exercising one of the rights listed above. Until 2014, this prohibition from dismissal was absolute: there was no exception stated in Directive 92/85/EC allowing a pregnant woman to be dismissed in exceptional cases not connected with her condition. The prohibition from the termination of the employment contract for as long as the rights related to the protection of parenthood are exercised (and some may be exercised for years) is not conducive to the employment of women. In 2014, the Labour Act envisaged that a pregnant woman or a woman who has given birth may be dismissed during the liquidation procedure due to business reasons, i.e., not related to pregnancy and motherhood. The same refers to fathers exercising the rights related to the protection of parenthood. Apart from this, the Insolvency Act of 2015 (amended in 2024) contains a provision in Article 191(3) which opens up the possibility of terminating pregnant women's employment contracts and employment contracts of fathers exercising the rights related to the protection of parenthood after filing for bankruptcy; this is indeed an exceptional case. According to this provision, after an employer has filed for bankruptcy, the administrator acting on behalf of the employer may terminate employment contracts, regardless of the duration of the contract and legal or contractual provisions on employee protection.

131. After the expiry of maternity and parental leave, adoption leave, half-time work, half-time work for the purpose of taking care of and nursing a child with severe developmental disabilities and the abeyance of employment relationship until the child's third year of age, the employee who has exercised one of these rights is entitled to be assigned to the same job they performed before exercising this right, and if the need for such a job no longer exists, the employer must offer them an employment contract for the performance of another appropriate job; the conditions must not be less favourable than the conditions at the post the employee had before exercising the right in question (Article 36 of the Labour Act).

B. Disabled Employees

132. In the Labour Act, the legislator has envisaged the prohibition of employment contract termination if the temporary incapacity is caused by an accident at work or an occupational disease (Article 38) and a prohibition of any adverse effect on the promotion and other benefits arising from employment if an employee was injured in an accident at work or has contracted an occupational disease (Article 39). The employees, regardless of whether they have been injured at work or elsewhere, regardless of whether their disease is occupational or not, are entitled to be reinstated to the same or equivalent post after their return from medical treatment or rehabilitation (Article 40(1) of the Labour Act). If an authorized person or body establishes that an employee suffers from an occupational work incapacity or that they are in immediate danger of incurring disability, the employer must take into consideration the expert opinion provided by the authorized person or body and offer the employee an employment contract for a job they are able to perform and which must, to the greatest possible extent, equal the job previously performed by the employee. In order to provide such a job, according to Article 41 of the Labour Act, the employer must adapt the job to the abilities of the employee, alter the working schedule, and do all they can to provide an appropriate job to the employee (this is referred to as reasonable accommodation). The employer may dismiss an employee who has reduced capacity for work due to an injury at work or an occupational disease and an employee with a disability only with the prior consent of the works council (Article 151(1)(3) of the Labour Act). The works council gives the employer consent to terminate an employment contract if the employer proves that they have done all they could to provide an appropriate job to the employee or if the employer proves that the employee has refused the offer of an employment contract for the performance of a job suited to their abilities, in accordance with the expert report and opinion of the authorized person or body. If the works council or shop steward who has the rights and obligations of the works council refuses to consent to the termination, the employer may file an appeal with the court or seek arbitration in order to supersede the works council's lack of consent; a judicial decision or an arbitration award may substitute such consent (Article 151(2–4) of the Labour Act).

133. An employee who has suffered an injury at work or has acquired an occupational disease and who was not returned to their post after the completion of their medical treatment and recovery is entitled to severance pay that is at least double the one they would normally get. An employee who has unjustifiably refused to accept a job offered to them does not have the right to double severance pay. An employee who suffers an injury at work or an occupational disease is to be given precedence in occupational training and education organized by the employer (Articles 42 and 43 of the Labour Act).

C. Apprentices

134. After completing the apprenticeship, an apprentice sits for an occupational examination, if so prescribed by a law, another regulation, collective agreement or employment regulations. The employer may give ordinary dismissal to an apprentice who has not passed the occupational examination (Article 58(3) of the Labour Act). In this regard, a note should be taken of provisions in the Civil Servants Act of 2023 (amended in 2024) stating that a civil servant shall be dismissed from civil service if they fail to pass a national professional examination within the prescribed period (Article 103(1)of the Civil Servants Act).

D. Members of Employee Representative Bodies

135. The works council members, candidates who stood for election for the works council and have not been elected for a period of three months following the election results, employees with a reduced work capacity as well as employees with disability, employees over 60 years of age and employee representatives in an employer's body may be dismissed only with the prior consent of the works council. If the works council does not grant or withhold its consent within eight days, it is presumed to have consented to the employer's decision. If the works council refuses to give its consent, the employer may, within fifteen days of the receipt of the statement of the refusal to give consent, ask that such consent be replaced by a judicial decision or an arbitration award. The Court of First Instance is obliged to rule in the case within thirty days from the day the action was filed (Article 151 of the Labour Act).

E. Shop Stewards

136. In addition to the subsidiary role the shop steward plays in the dismissal procedure when they assume the role of the works council if the works council has not been established, the trade unions have been given by the Labour Act a primary power to participate in the dismissal procedure. According to Article 188(1) of the Labour Act, during the shop steward's term of office and for six months after the end of this term, the shop steward's employment contract may not be terminated without the prior consent of the trade union. The shop steward may not be placed in a less favourable position than other employees in any other way if the trade union has not given its consent to that effect. If the trade union does not give or withhold its consent within eight days, it is presumed to have consented to the employer's decision. If the trade union refuses to give consent to dismissal, the employer may, within fifteen days of the receipt of the trade union's observations, request that such consent be replaced by a judicial decision. At least one shop steward is entitled to this protection; the maximum number of shop stewards who enjoy this protection is determined by applying *mutatis mutandis* the provisions of the Labour Act on the number of the works council members.

V. Collective Dismissals

137. According to Article 127 of the Labour Act, when an employer has a redundancy of at least twenty employees whose employment contacts are to be terminated within a period of ninety days, irrespective of the method of termination, and if at least five of these employees are to be dismissed for business reasons, the employer must consult the works council in order to try to eliminate the need for dismissals. For the purpose of complying with the duty to consult, the employer must give the works council all the relevant information: reasons for the planned redundancies, total number of employees, number and categories of employees who are most likely to be made redundant and whose employment contracts will be terminated, the criteria proposed for the selection of the employees to be made redundant, the amount and method for calculating severance pay, and other payments to the employees and measures designed to alleviate the consequences of redundancy for employees. The employer must notify the competent public employment service about the consultation with the works council, and the notification has to contain the information on the duration of consultation with the works council, outcomes and conclusions resulting therefrom, with a statement of works council if s/he has received it (Article 127(5) of the Labour Act).

138. According to Article 127(4) of the Labour Act, the works council may submit to the competent public employment service and the employer its comments and suggestions. The employer is not allowed to dismiss the employees who are to be dismissed as redundant under the collective redundancy plan within a period of thirty days from the submission of the notification to the competent public employment service. Furthermore, the competent employment service may order the suspension of the dismissal of all or some employees who are to be made redundant;

this suspension must not stand longer than thirty days if s/he is able to ensure the continuation of employment for the employees during this extended period (Article 128 of the Labour Act).

Chapter 7. Non-competition Covenant, Employee Inventions

139. Articles 101 through 106 of the Labour Act provide for a statutory and contractual prohibition of competition. An employee must not, without the approval of his or her employer, conclude business transactions, for their own account or for the account of others, in the field of activity of their employer ('statutory prohibition of competition'). If the employee fails to honour this prohibition, the employer may claim compensation for the damage from the employee or may demand that the business transaction be considered concluded for the employer's account or that the employee surrender to the employer the profit earned from such transaction or transfer to the employer any claims for profits earned from such a transaction. The employer's right expires three months after the date on which the employer learnt that the business transaction had been concluded; in any case, it expires five years from the date when the transaction was concluded. If, at the time the employment commences, the employer is aware of the fact that the employee was engaged in business activities and did not demand the employee to cease engaging in such activities, the employer is considered to have given the employee approval for engagement in these activities. The employer may revoke the approval, complying in this respect with the time limit prescribed or agreed upon for the termination of an employment contract. In line with the jurisprudence of the VSRH, the failure to honour the prohibition of competition constitutes just cause for extraordinary dismissal of the employee (VSRH, Revr-116/07 of 16 May 2007). However, the mere fact that an employee has established a company registered for the same activities that the employer is engaged in does not constitute a violation of the statutory prohibition of competition, provided the employee has not actually engaged in these activities (VSRH, Revr-29/05 of 9 February 2005).

140. The employment contract may include a provision on the so-called contractual prohibition of competition or a separate contract may be concluded to that effect. The employer and the employee may stipulate that, for a certain time after the termination of the employment contract, the employee must not enter into employment with another person who is competing on the market with the employer and that the employee must not conclude business transactions that constitute competition with the employer, neither for their own account nor for the account of others. Such contracts must not be valid for longer than two years after the date of the termination of employment. They must be concluded in written form. The contract is not binding on the employee if the purpose of the contract is not to protect the legitimate business interests of the employer or if, taking into account the scope, duration and purpose of the prohibition and the legitimate business interests of the employer, the contract disproportionately limits the career of the employee. The contract is rendered null and void if it is concluded by a minor employee or by an employee who, at the time the contract is concluded, is receiving a salary amounting to less than the average salary in Croatia; in these cases, the nullity of the contractual prohibition of competition may not be invoked by the employer. The contractual prohibition of competition is binding on an employee only if the employer has undertaken a contractual obligation to pay compensation to the employee for the duration of the prohibition, amounting to at least half of the average salary paid to the employee in the period of three months prior to the termination of the employment contract.

Salary compensation must be paid by the employer until the fifteenth day of the current month for the previous month. If part of the employee's salary is intended to cover costs related to the performance of work, the compensation may be proportionately reduced. If employees terminate their employment contract through the extraordinary termination procedure because the employer has seriously violated an obligation arising from the employment contract, the contractual prohibition of competition ceases to apply if the employee declares in writing, within a month of the date of the employment contract termination, that he or she does not consider himself or herself bound by this contract. The contractual prohibition of competition ceases to apply if the employer terminates the employment contract without just cause, as stipulated by the Labour Act, unless the employer notifies the employee, within fifteen days of the termination of the contract, that they will pay compensation to the employee, for the duration of the contractual prohibition of competition; the compensation amounts to the average monthly salary paid to the employee in the period of three months prior to the termination of the employment contract. The employer may be released from the obligation to pay the compensation if they notify the employee in writing that they have waived the contractual prohibition of competition. The waiver of the contractual prohibition of competition releases the employer from any obligation to pay compensation after three months following the date on which the waiver was submitted to the employee. Where only a contractual penalty has been provided for a violation of the contractual prohibition of competition, the employer may, in accordance with the general provisions of the civil obligations law, claim only this penalty and not the fulfilment of the obligation or higher compensation for the damage. A contractual penalty may also be agreed upon instead of the employer's obligation to pay salary compensation for the duration of the contractual prohibition of competition if, at the moment of conclusion of such agreement, the employee was receiving a salary exceeding the average salary in Croatia (Article 106 of the Labour Act).

141. The rights of employers and employees relating to the employees' inventions and to the technical innovations proposed by an employee are regulated by Articles 98 through 100 of the Labour Act. An employee must inform his or her employer of any inventions made at work or in relation to the work. The employee must treat all the information about the invention as confidential business information and must not pass it to a third party without prior approval of the employer. The invention is the property of the employer, and the employee is entitled to compensation established by a collective agreement, an employment contract or a special contract. If compensation is not established in this manner, appropriate compensation can be established by the court. It is worth mentioning that the invention created by the assigned worker is the property of the user undertaking, and the assigned worker is entitled to a reward established by the special contract (Article 98(4) of the Labour Act). An employee must inform the employer about an invention even if it was not made at work or in relation to the work, if this invention is related to the employer's activity, and must make the employer a written offer to transfer to the employer their rights in relation to this invention. The employer must respond to the employee's offer within a period of one month. The provisions of the civil obligations law governing the right of pre-emption apply *mutatis mutandis* to the transfer of the right to an invention. If the employer agrees to use a technical innovation proposed by an employee, the employer must compensate the employee; the amount of the compensation is established by a collective agreement, an employment contract or a special contract. If compensation is not established in this manner, appropriate compensation can be established by the court.

Chapter 8. Settlement of Individual Labour Disputes

142. Individual labour disputes stem from the rights related to individual employment relationships. In individual labour disputes, it is possible to claim declaratory protection (a finding that a right based on the employment or the employment itself exists), enforceable protection (a judgment compelling the respondent to take certain action) or the protection whereby a legal right or relationship is established, altered or terminated (enacting a legal change, e.g., judicial termination of the employment contract).[2] The ordinary legal relief is recourse to the courts, i.e., a legal suit. The Civil Procedure Act of 1977 (last amended in 2023) and the Labour Act govern the procedure in labour disputes. Municipal courts (the first instance labour court in Zagreb and ordinary civil law courts in other parts of Croatia since there are no labour courts elsewhere) have general jurisdiction *ratione materiae* for labour disputes. In exceptional cases, the legislator has envisaged that a County Court or a Commercial Court have jurisdiction *ratione materiae*. County courts thus have subject-matter jurisdiction in ruling on court injunctions against illegal strikes and lock-outs (collective labour disputes). Commercial courts adjudicate in labour disputes where one of the parties is in bankruptcy proceedings, in disputes between the ship crews and shipping companies, or a floor manager and the company they work for, and between the ship captains and shipping companies (Article 164 of the Maritime Code of 2004, last amended in 2019), and in labour disputes between members of the board of directors of a company and the company on remuneration arising from managerial contracts. The Administrative Court of Croatia has jurisdiction over labour disputes in civil service based on Article 42(5)of the Civil Servants Act of 2023 (amended in 2024). This court also has jurisdiction over disputes related to the protection of the rights of the directors of public institutions in the matter of their appointment when they are appointed by the Government of Croatia, the head of the competent civil service or a representative body of a local and regional self-government unit (Article 42(3) of the Act on Institutions of 1993, last amended in 2022). This is the case when the separate law or the founding act of the public institution prescribes such appointment. In other cases, the municipal courts (the first instance labour court in Zagreb and ordinary civil law courts in other parts of Croatia since there are no labour courts elsewhere) have jurisdiction over the disputes related to the protection of the rights of the directors of public institutions in the matter or their appointment.

143. Mediation and arbitration are alternatives to the judicial resolution of individual and collective labour disputes. The mediation procedure is regulated in the Mediation Act of 2023. The Arbitration Act of 2001 contains general provisions that apply, *inter alia,* to arbitration in labour disputes. The jurisdiction of the court of arbitration is determined by a written contract (Article 6(2) of the Arbitration Act), which means that an employment contract may contain an arbitration clause. For the so-called compulsory arbitration in collective labour disputes (disputes on the

2. More details in M. Dika, Ž. Potočnjak & V. Gotovac, *Radni Sporovi*, in *Radni odnosi u Republici Hrvatskoj*, Zagreb, 2007, pp. 649–770.

definition of tasks that must not be disrupted during a strike and lock-out), *see* paragraph 189. The only restriction to domestic arbitration (in the territory of Croatia) is the dispositive nature of the right that is the subject of the dispute. These must be the rights that the parties may freely dispose of (Article 3(1) of the Arbitration Act). However, in foreign arbitration cases, in addition to the dispositive nature of the right that is the subject of the dispute, the Croatian courts must lack exclusive international jurisdiction (Article 3(2) of the Arbitration Act). The Arbitration Act allows parties to challenge the arbitration judgments by a legal suit (Articles 36 and 43(1) of the Arbitration Act). Some legal theorists warn of a low level of general legal knowledge in the sphere of alternative ways to resolve disputes and of many vague and unclear provisions in the legislative framework for these instruments.

144. According to the Civil Procedure Act, labour disputes are adjudicated in the first instance by a single judge; the reviews are, as a rule, performed by a panel of five judges. As for legal representation in labour disputes, the Civil Procedure Act envisages an exception to the rule that only an attorney at law may represent a party. An employee may be represented in a labour dispute by a person employed in the trade union of which the employee is a member or in the trade union association this trade union is affiliated with, while the employer may be represented by a person employed in the employers' association of which the employer is a member or a higher-level employers' association which includes the association the employer belongs to (Article 434a of the Civil Procedure Act).

145. The Labour Act envisages two procedures whereby judicial protection of the rights related to employment may be obtained: one pertains to the obligation to first seek relief from the employer (the legislator has envisaged exceptions where it is possible to go to court directly, without first seeking relief from the employer. This issue will be dealt with in greater detail below) within preclusive time limits; the failure to comply with these limits results in the forfeiture of the right to legal (judicial) protection. The other procedure pertains to the protection from harassment and sexual harassment (also known as the protection of the employees' dignity; for more details, *see* next paragraph). Article 133 of the Labour Act stipulates that an employee must submit to the employer a document called a request for the protection of a right before going to court. An employee who considers that their employer has violated any of their rights arising from employment may, within fifteen days following the receipt of a decision violating this right or following the day when they became aware of such a violation, request from the employer to allow them to exercise this right. If the employer does not comply with the employee's request within fifteen days from the date of the service of the request, the employee has fifteen days to seek judicial protection before the court that has jurisdiction in respect of the right that has been violated. The employee who has failed to submit this request to the employer is precluded from seeking judicial protection before the court, except where the employee seeks damages or has other financial claims arising from employment. When a law, other regulations, collective agreements or employment regulations provide for alternative dispute resolution, the time limit of fifteen days for filing a request to the court starts running on the date when the alternative dispute resolution procedure ends.

Legal theory entertains opposite views of the constitutionality of the provision compelling an employee to first seek relief from their employer with the failure to do so within preclusive time limits resulting in the forfeiture of the right to seek legal (judicial) protection. Some scholars argue the provision is unconstitutional because it restricts the right to free access to courts. Others believe this is a form of preventing a dispute that would otherwise be adjudicated by a court or in the course of arbitration. A similar obligation to attempt to solve the dispute amicably is envisaged in Article 186a of the Civil Procedure Act of 1991 (last amended in 2023) for legal disputes where the respondent is Croatia in the capacity of an employer:

> A person who intends to file a complaint against the Republic of Croatia is obliged before filing the complaint to approach the competent public prosecutor's office with a request for an amicable solution to the dispute … If the request is not accepted, or no decision is made on it within three months of its filling, the applicant may file a complaint with the competent court. The court shall dismiss a complaint against the Republic of Croatia filed before a decision on the request for an amicable solution of the dispute has been rendered.

146. In addition to the procedure that precedes the judicial protection of the rights arising from employment described above, Article 134 of the Labour Act regulates the procedure for the protection of the employees' dignity against harassment and sexual harassment. The procedures and measures for the protection of the employees' dignity against harassment or sexual harassment can be governed by a *lex specialis*, a collective agreement, and an agreement between the works council and the employer or in the employment regulations. An employer employing at least twenty employees must appoint a person (the confidential counsellor) and an employer who employs more than seventy-five employees is obliged to appoint two persons of different genders who, in addition to him/her, are authorized to receive and resolve complaints related to the protection of employees' dignity against harassment and sexual harassment. The employer or confidential counsellor must examine the complaint and take all the necessary measures appropriate in each particular case to put a stop to the harassment or sexual harassment. They must do so within the time limits prescribed by a collective agreement, an agreement between the works council and the employer or the employment regulations, and not later than eight days from the day the complaint was filed, if they have established that harassment has occurred. If the employer has failed to take measures to prevent harassment or sexual harassment within that time limit, or if the measures they have taken are clearly inappropriate, the employee who is a victim of harassment or sexual harassment has the right to stop working until they are offered protection, provided that they have sought protection from a competent court within the following eight days. If circumstances occur which make it improbable to expect that the employer will protect the employee's dignity, the employee is not obliged to file a complaint with the employer and has the right to stop working, provided that they have sought protection in the competent court and notified the employer thereof, within eight days of the date when they stopped working. During the period off work, the employee is entitled to salary compensation in the amount they would have received if they had worked. However, the employer may request the refund of salary compensation in the event of a valid judicial decision ruling that the employee's dignity was not violated, i.e., when the employee failed to prove harassment/sexual harassment (Article 134(9) of the Labour Act). All the information collected in the procedure for the protection of employees' dignity is confidential. A conduct by an employee that constitutes harassment or sexual harassment is a violation of the employment obligations. The efforts of an employee to oppose the conduct that constitutes harassment or sexual harassment are not a violation of the employment obligation and must not be cause for discrimination. The notion of harassment, as well as sexual harassment, is defined in the Anti-discrimination Act of 2008 (amended in 2012), modelled on the definitions used in the EU non-discrimination directives.

147. Burden of proof in labour disputes is regulated by Article 135 of the Labour Act. If there is a labour dispute, the burden of proof lies with the person who considers that their rights arising from employment have been violated or who has instituted legal action unless the Labour Act or another law stipulates otherwise. The provisions of the Anti-discrimination Act apply to the transfer of the burden of proof in anti-discrimination cases. More specifically, under Article 20 of the Anti-discrimination Act, the claimant must prove prima facie discrimination and then the respondent must prove that there has been no discrimination. The same applies to disputes relating to unfavourable treatment (victimization) of an employee as a result of an action taken because of suspected corruption or a report of suspected corruption submitted by this employee to responsible persons or competent authorities. If the employee, according to Article 135(2) of the Labour Act, is able to establish facts that indicate that they have been treated less favourably or that their rights arising from employment have been violated, the burden of proof is shifted to the employer who must prove that the employee has not been put at a disadvantage compared to other employees or that their rights arising from employment have not been violated. In case of a dispute related to dismissal, the burden of proof of the existence of a justified reason for dismissal lies with the employer. The burden of proof lies with an employee only if an employee resorts to the extraordinary termination of the employment contract. In case of a dispute related to working time, if an employer does not keep records of employees and their working time in a way prescribed by the Minister's Ordinance, the burden of proof lies with the employer.

148. The Civil Procedure Act stipulates that labour disputes must be dealt with urgently (Article 434(1)). Article 434(4) and (5) of the same Act envisages the so-called instructive deadlines for the completion of the first instance proceedings (six months from the date when the legal suit was filed) and the second instance proceedings (the appeal must be ruled on within thirty days of its receipt). The deadline for the appeal is fifteen days (Article 348(1) of the Civil Procedure Act). The VSRH may review the cases. As a rule, the parties in the dispute may file a review against the judgment rendered in the second instance if the Supreme Court has allowed it. Among others, the VSRH will allow it if the party makes it probable that in the first and second instance proceedings, due to particularly serious violations of the provisions of the civil procedure or incorrect application of substantive law, a fundamental human right guaranteed by the Constitution of the Republic of Croatia and the European Convention for the Protection of Human Rights and Fundamental Freedoms has been violated and that the party, if possible, had already referred to these violations in the lower-level proceedings (Articles 382 and 385a of the Civil Procedure Act).

149. The Act on International Private Law of 2017 (amended in 2023) refers to Regulation (EC) No. 593/2008 of the European Parliament and of the Council of 17 June 2008 on the law applicable to contractual obligations (Rome I).

Part II. Collective Labour Law

Chapter 1. Freedom of Association

150. Croatia is bound by ILO Convention No. 87 concerning freedom of association and protection of the right to organize and ILO Convention No. 98 concerning the application of the principles of the right to organize and to bargain collectively. The rights guaranteed by the above-mentioned conventions are guaranteed by the Constitution of the Republic of Croatia as well, which guarantees freedom of association in Article 43:

> Everyone shall be guaranteed the right to freedom of association for the purposes of protection of common interests or promotion of social, economic, political, national, cultural and other convictions and aims. For this purpose, anyone may freely form trade unions and other associations, join them or leave them, in compliance with law. The right to free association shall be restricted by the prohibition of any violent threat to the democratic constitutional order and the independence, unity, and territorial integrity of the Republic of Croatia.

Furthermore, Article 60 of the Constitution of the Republic of Croatia reads as follows:

> In order to protect their economic and social interests, all employees shall be entitled to form trade unions and they shall be free to join and leave them. Trade unions may form their federations and join international trade union organizations. The formation of trade unions in the armed forces and the police may be restricted by law. Employers shall be entitled to form associations and they shall be free to join and leave them.

These restrictions to the freedom of association envisaged by the Constitution are contained in the Service in the Armed Forces Act of 2013 (last amended in 2024). Its Article 15(1) prohibits only active-duty service personnel from joining trade unions; non-combat personnel in the Armed Forces may freely join trade unions. Police officers are entitled to join trade unions, according to Article 40(1) of the Police Act of 2011 (last amended in 2023).

151. Detailed provisions on the employees' rights to join trade unions and the employers' rights to form associations are contained in Articles 165 through 191 of the Labour Act. These provisions guarantee the freedom to form trade unions and employers' associations without any prior approval, as the approval requirement would be counter to freedom of association. Furthermore, the voluntary nature of membership in an association is guaranteed. The executive branch of the government may not temporarily ban or disband an association (Article 167 of the Labour Act). Any discrimination based on membership in an association is prohibited, as stipulated by Article 166(2) of the Labour Act; Article 1(1) of the Anti-discrimination Act lists the prohibited grounds for discrimination and includes membership in a trade union. Freedom of association would be impossible without such a prohibition. The Criminal Code of 2011 (last amended in 2024) envisages imprisonment of up to one year for a person who denies or restricts the right to establish trade unions and other associations to join or leave them in line with the law (Article 129). The fact that the reports of this criminal offence have been extremely rare indicates that the prevention of the establishment of trade unions is not widespread. An analysis of the activities of the ILO Committee on Freedom of Association leads to the same conclusion: it has been called upon to rule on several cases related to complaints from Croatia. The complaints were related to the interference in the trade union activities and with trade union assets, violation of the right to strike, discrimination based on trade union activities, obstacles to the registration of a confederation and the attitude of the Government that the salaries in the public sector cannot be settled freely through collective bargaining, as a part of the Government's stabilization policy.

Chapter 2. Trade Unions and the Employers' Associations

152. About 26% of the employees in Croatia are trade union members. Although the trade union density is relatively high, this is due to the highly unionized public sector. On the contrary, in the private sector, the trade union density is lower, in particular in small companies where it is significantly below 10%. The Croatian trade union scene in Croatia is heterogeneous and fragmented. According to Article 171 of the Labour Act, a trade union may be established by at least ten adult persons with legal capacity. An employers' association may be established by at least three legal entities or adult persons with legal capacity. A total of 334 trade unions active either throughout Croatia or in at least two or more counties, and 296 trade unions active in only one of the counties have been registered in the association registry. Unlike the employees who are members of a large number of various trade unions, the employers have formed a relatively small number of employers' associations. The first voluntary employers' association was established in Croatia as late as 1993. To date, fifty-six employers' associations active throughout Croatia or in two or more countries and six employers' associations active in only one county have been registered in Croatia. A higher-level association may be established by at least two associations. In Croatia, there are twenty-five higher-level trade union associations and three higher-level employers' associations. The representativeness of the higher-level trade union associations has been regulated by the Act on the Representativeness of Employers' Associations and Trade Unions of 2014 (amended in 2015). There are three representative trade union centrals (Decision of the Representativeness Commission of 16 June 2023, Official Gazette No. 120/2023): Independent Trade Unions of Croatia, Union of Autonomous Trade Unions of Croatia and Association of Croatian Trade Unions. The Union of Autonomous Trade Unions of Croatia and the Independent Trade Unions of Croatia are members of the European Trade Union Confederation (ETUC) and the International Trade Union Confederation (ITUC). The higher-level employers' associations are the Croatian Employers' Association (the only representative employers' association), the Independent Employers' Associations Federation and the Croatian Industry and Entrepreneurs Confederation. The Croatian Employers' Association is a member of the International Organization of Employers (IOE) and BusinessEurope.

153. An association or a higher-level association must have the articles of association based on and adopted according to the principles of democratic representation and democratic exercise of its members' will. The articles of association must, *inter alia*, include the provisions identifying the bodies authorized to conclude collective agreements and specifying the requirements and procedures for industrial actions. Entering into collective agreements must be specified in the articles of association as one of the purposes of the association.

154. The Labour Act contains provisions on the associations' assets (Articles 181 and 182 of the Labour Act) guaranteeing their financial independence. The associations may acquire assets by collecting enrolment and membership fees, by purchase, from donations or in any other legal manner, without any prior authorization. Real estate and moveable assets of the associations necessary for their meetings, educational activities, and libraries may not be subject to execution. If an association splits, or if a substantial number of its members create a separate association, the assets of this association are divided proportionately to the number of former members of the original association who have joined the newly founded entities unless otherwise provided by the articles of association, a contract or other agreement. If an association ceases to operate, its assets are disposed of in the manner prescribed by its articles of association. Its assets may not be allocated to its members. The guarantee of prohibition of control over the trade unions is contained in Article 183 of the Labour Act. According to this provision, employers and their associations must not exercise control over the establishment and operations of trade unions or their higher-level associations; they must not finance or in any other way support trade unions or their higher-level associations in order to exercise such control. The prohibition of control is also applicable to the relations between the trade unions and their higher-level associations and the employers and their associations. Judicial protection of membership rights is guaranteed by Article 184 of the Labour Act: members of an association may seek judicial protection if their rights guaranteed by the articles of association or other rules have been violated.

155. Judicial protection of the right to associate is guaranteed by Article 185 of the Labour Act. According to this provision, an association or a higher-level association may petition the court to prohibit the actions that violate the right of employees and employers to associate. An association or a higher-level association may claim compensation for the damage suffered as a result of the prohibited activities. The prohibition of unequal treatment on the grounds of membership in a trade union or participation in trade union activities is guaranteed by Article 186 of the Labour Act: employees must not be placed in a less favourable position than other employees on the ground of their membership in a trade union. It is, in particular, prohibited to offer an employment contract to an employee on condition that they refrain from joining a trade union or that they leave a trade union, to terminate an employment contract or place an employee in a less favourable position than other employees in some other way because of their membership in a trade union or participation in trade union activities after working hours or during working hours, subject to the consent of the employer. The employer must not take into consideration membership in a trade union and participation in trade union activities when deciding whether or not to offer an employment contract assigning an employee to a particular job or to a particular workplace, specialist training, promotion, pay, social benefits and termination of an employment contract. Employers, chief executives or other bodies and employer's representatives must not use coercion to favour or impede any trade union.

156. The rights of trade union representatives and shop stewards are guaranteed by Articles 187 and 188 of the Labour Act. Trade unions decide autonomously on the methods of their representation before the employer. Trade unions that have at least five members employed with an employer may appoint or elect one or more trade union representatives or commissioners to represent them before this employer. Trade union representatives or shop stewards have the right to protect and promote the interests of trade union members in their dealings with the employer. The employer must make it possible for a trade union representative or shop steward to exercise, duly and effectively, their right and must provide them with access to information necessary for the exercise of this right. A trade union representative or a shop steward must exercise their right at the time and in a manner that will not adversely affect the employer's business. The trade union must inform the employer in writing about the appointment of a trade union representative or shop steward. A trade union representative has all the rights and obligations that a shop steward has, except for the shop stewards' rights and obligations arising from employment or related to employment. Shop stewards enjoy special protection: while they serve as shop stewards and for six months after the termination of their duty without prior consent of the trade union, their employment contracts may not be terminated, and they may not be assigned to another job or be placed in a less favourable position than his/her previous working conditions or than other employees. If the trade union does not give or withhold its consent within eight days, it is presumed to have consented to the employer's decision. If the trade union refuses to consent to a dismissal, the employer may, within fifteen days of the receipt of the trade union's observations, request that such consent be replaced by a judicial decision. This protection can be afforded to at least one shop steward; the maximum number of shop stewards who enjoy protection is determined by applying *mutatis mutandis* the provisions of the Labour Act on the number of the works council members.

157. Trade union fees are regulated by Article 189 of the Labour Act. At the request of and in accordance with the instructions of the trade union, and with the prior written consent of the employee who is a trade union member, the employer will calculate and withhold from the employee's salary the relevant trade union fees and will regularly transfer these fees to the trade union's account.

158. A trade union and employers' association may cease their activities: (1) if this is decided by a body of the association authorized by the articles of association to make this decision; (2) if the highest body of the association has not been convened during a period which is twice as long as the period specified by the articles of association; (3) if the number of its members falls below the number required for the establishment of an association by the Labour Act (based on the report of the highest body of the association submitted to the body authorized for registration); (4) if the association's activities have been banned by a court (Articles 190(1) and 190(3)of the Labour Act). The ban on the activities of an association is regulated by Article 191 of the Labour Act: 'The activities of an association shall be banned by a decision of a county court which has territorial jurisdiction in the area where an association has its seat, if the activities of an association are contrary to the Constitution and the law. The proceedings to ban the association's activities shall be initiated upon a motion by the body authorized for the registration or by the authorized public prosecutor. The judgment banning the activities of an association must include a statement of reasons indicating the activities which led to the ban.'

159. The central body through which social dialogue and partnership are conducted in Croatia is the Economic and Social Council; it also serves as an advisory body of the Government of Croatia. It is a tripartite body comprising the representatives of the trade unions, the employers' associations and the Government. It is established under an agreement between the Government and the representative trade unions and employers' associations. Article 221(3) of the Labour Act defines the powers of the Economic and Social Council. The Council provides opinions (with a statement of reasons) to the minister responsible for labour regarding any issues in the conclusion and application of collective agreements; it makes proposals to the Government, employers and trade unions or to their associations and higher-level associations aimed at achieving a coordinated price and salary policy; establishes a list of potential mediators (who conduct the compulsory mediation procedure before a strike – *see* paragraph 189); establishes a list of potential arbitrators and arbitration board members; provides opinions on the draft legislation in the area of labour and social security, etc.

160. In addition to voluntary employers' associations, there is the Croatian Chamber of Economy; in line with the Croatian Chamber of Economy Act of 2021, membership is compulsory for all legal persons engaged in business and established in Croatia. The Croatian Chamber of Economy cannot be a party to any collective agreements, as only voluntary associations of employers may sign such agreements. The basic tasks of the Croatian Chamber of Economy are: representation, coordination and protection of the shared interests of its members before state bodies; participation in the structuring of the economic system and shaping economic policy measures; participation in the restructuring of the economy; developing entrepreneurial initiatives; promotion of the Croatian economy abroad, etc. Legal entities engaged in trades and crafts in the territory of Croatia, individual tradespersons and companies engaged in trades and crafts must be members of the Croatian Chamber of Trades and Crafts (Trades and Crafts Act of 2013, last amended in 2020).

Chapter 3. Institutionalized Forms of Employee Participation

§1. Works Councils

161. The Labour Act of 1995, which entered into force on 1 January 1996, first introduced the legal obligation for employee participation based on the German model. The passing of the Act caused a furore precisely because of the way it regulated employee participation; there were concerns that this signalled a return to the workers' self-management caused by the perception of employee participation as a relic of the socialist regime.

162. The current Labour Act of 2014 (last amended in 2023) regulates the issue of works councils in Articles 140 through 162. The employees working for an employer with at least twenty employees have the right to elect a works council in order to be able to participate in the decision-making process on issues related to their economic and social entitlements and interests. Employees in public administration bodies do not enjoy this right. This is a right, not an obligation, of the employees. If the employees fail to elect a works council, its powers will be assumed by the shop steward. The procedure for the establishment of a works council is initiated at the proposal of a trade union or at least 20% of the employees who work for an employer. The number of members of the works council is based on the number of employees working for an employer, as follows:

- up to 75 employees: 1 representative;
- 76–250 employees: 3 representatives;
- 251–500 employees: 5 representatives;
- 501–750 employees: 7 representatives;
- 751–1,000 employees: 9 representatives.

For every further 1,000 employees, the number of members of the works council is increased by two. Trade union members may sit on the works council, and in practice, that is most often the case. In the process of the election of the works council members, all organizational units and groups of employees (by gender, age, qualification, jobs they perform, etc.) must be equally represented. If the employer's business is organized in several organizational units, employees may establish several works councils in order to ensure adequate involvement of all the employees. A general works council is established only if the works councils are established in all organizational units; it comprises representatives of the works councils of all organizational units. A works council is elected for a term of four years. In principle, all employees have the right to vote for and be voted into the works council. This right belongs even to the employees who are legal minors and who do not have the right to vote until their majority. However, members of the boards of directors and of supervisory boards, their family members, and the representatives of an employer (natural person) authorized to exercise employer's rights and obligations arising from employment do not have the right to vote for and to be voted into the works council. An electoral committee is established to organize elections. The same persons who can initiate the procedure for the election of a works council (trade unions whose members work for the employer or a group of employees which enjoys the support of at least 20% of the employees who work for the employer) may propose lists of candidates for employee representatives in the works council. The elections are valid if at least one-third of the employees with voting rights have actually voted (Article 17 of the Ordinance on the Procedure for Electing Works Council of 2016, last amended in 2020). If only one representative is to be elected, the candidate who has received the majority of votes cast must be elected. If two or more candidates receive the same number of votes, the candidate who has more years of continuous service is elected. If three or more representatives are to be elected, the number of elected representatives from each list is determined by applying D'Hondt's method of proportional representation.

163. Unlike trade unions, which may use pressure, such as strikes or other industrial actions, to increase the level of legal protection of employees, the works councils must not participate in the organization or performance of strikes or other industrial actions, nor may they in any other way interfere in a collective labour dispute which may result in such an action. The works councils are a different conduit for employee protection. The protection they afford to the employees hinges on their right to intervene and change decisions made by the employers. The Labour Act lists the employers' decisions that are taken with the participation of the works council. The works councils have three basic functions: the right to be informed of some decisions taken by the employer, the right to consult the employer in the process of making decisions on the issues stipulated by the law and the right of co-decision with the employer on the issues stipulated by the law. The employer is obliged to inform the works council at least every three months about: (1) the current business situation and results, the work organization; (2) the expected development of business activities and their effect on the economic and social status of the employees; (3) the trends and changes in salaries; (4) the extent of and the reasons for the introduction of overtime work; (5) number and category of employees, the structure of the employees (the number of fixed-term employees, employees at alternative workplaces, workers assigned by temporary employment agencies, workers temporary posted to/from associated company, etc.), and employment policy; (6) the number and type of employees to whom they have a written consent to additional job; (7) health and safety at work and measures taken in order to improve working conditions; (8) outcomes of inspections of work and safety at work conditions; and (9) other issues of particular importance for the economic and social status of the employees. Another mechanism through which the works council interfere in the employer's autonomous decision-making is the duty of the employer to consult the works council before making decisions that will affect the employees' position. Such important decisions include, in particular, decisions on: the adoption of employment regulations (*see* paragraph 28), employment policy, dismissal (for more details on the role of the works council in the dismissal cases, *see* paragraphs 126 through 130), measures related to health and safety at work, the introduction of new technologies and changes of the work organization and methods, annual leave plans, work schedules, night work, the compensation for inventions and technical innovations, collective redundancies and transfer of an undertaking, business or part of an undertaking or business and the transfer of employment contracts to a new employer and the impact of any such transfers on employees and appointment of a person who is authorized to receive and resolve complaints related to the protection of the dignity of workers against harassment and sexual harassment. If the employer has failed to consult the works council, any decisions are null and void.

The highest level of interference of the works council in the autonomy of the employer is the obligation of the employer to seek the works council's consent for the decisions stipulated by the law. The following decisions cannot be made by the employer without the prior consent of the works council: (1) dismissing the works council members; (2) dismissing candidates who stood for election in the works council but were not elected, for a period of three months following the election results; (3) dismissing employees with a reduced ability to work, or dismissing disabled employees; (4) dismissing employees over sixty years of age; (5) dismissing the employee representatives in an employer's board (such as supervisory board or board of directors); (6) including pregnant employees as well as other employees protected against dismissal in collective redundancy except in cases when the employer has initiated or is conducting liquidation proceedings; (7) collecting, processing and using data about employees and disseminating such data to third persons; (8) appointing a person who will be authorized to supervise whether personal data about employees are collected, processed, used or disseminated to third persons in accordance with the provisions of the Labour Act. The works council is presumed to have consented to the employer's decision if it has not taken a position (i.e., granted or refused its consent) within eight days. If the works council refuses to give its consent, the employer may, within fifteen days of the receipt of the statement on the refusal, request that such consent be replaced by a judicial decision or an arbitration award.

164. In the context of workers participation at the supranational level, it is worth mentioning that in order to bring the Croatian legislation in line with the EU *acquis*, two separate pieces of legislation have been adopted: the Act on European Works Councils of 2014 (amended in 2017), and the Act on the Introduction of European Company – Societas Europaea and European Economic Interest Grouping (EEIG) of 2007 (amended in 2015).

165. There are other forms of employee participation, in addition to the works councils: the employees' meetings and the employee participation in the employer's board, such as the supervisory board and the board of directors (*see* paragraphs 167–169). According to Article 163 of the Labour Act, the employees who work for an employer must meet at least twice a year at regular intervals; these meetings are venues at which the employees are kept informed about all the relevant developments and where they can discuss the functioning of the works council. These meetings are convened by the works council upon prior consultation with the employer. If no works council has been established, the employees' meetings have to be convened by the employer. Even if a works council has been established, the employer may convene an employees' meeting if the employer considers that there is a need. The employer must consult the works council about it.

§2. Employee Participation on the Employer's Boards (Supervisory Board, Board of Directors)

166. Since 2001, the Labour Act stipulates that employees may take part in the work of the supervisory board of their company. Until 2008, there was a two-tier structure in the companies: the management board, which was in charge of managing the company, was separated from the supervisory board, which was in charge of supervising the management of the company. After 1 April 2008, with the entry into force of an amendment to the Commercial Companies Act, the companies can opt for a single-tier system in addition to the existing two-tier system: the board of directors may both manage and supervise the management of the company. Therefore, the Labour Act in its Article 164 states that in the companies or cooperatives which have a body that supervises business activities (a supervisory board, a board of directors or other appropriate body) and in public institutions, an employee representative must sit on such a board. They are appointed and recalled by the works council. If no works council has been established, the employee representative is elected from among the employees who work for the employer. They can be recalled by the employees. The election and recall are by direct and secret ballot, in the manner prescribed by the Labour Act for the election of a one-member works council (*see* paragraph 163). The employee representative appointed or elected in this way has the same legal position as other appointed members of the organ. Thus, since 2010, the law stipulates that in a public limited company, one of the members of the supervisory board or one of the members of the board of directors must be a representative of the employees. As regards limited liability companies, some have and some do not have a supervisory board; the Commercial Companies Act of 1993 (last amended in 2023) stipulates when a limited liability company must have a supervisory board. If there is a supervisory body, one or more of its members must be representatives of the employees. Under the Cooperative Partnership Act of 2011 (amended in 2019), a cooperative that has twenty or more members must have a supervisory board. One of its members must be a representative of the employees. The same principle applies to public institutions: one of the members of the board of the public institution must be a representative of the employees working in the institution (Articles 80(1) and 80(2) of the Act on Public Institutions of 1993, amended in 2022).

167. The employee representative need not be an employee of the company; it can be any other person the employees have appointed as their representative. This will not be the case when a works council has not been established and when, consequently, the employee representative is elected by the employees in a direct and secret ballot. In that case, they can only elect a person employed by the employer. Under Article 45(4) of the Credit Institutions Act of 2013 (last amended in 2022), the employees of a credit institution (banks, savings banks, building societies) may not serve as members of the supervisory board of the credit institution.

168. The employer is charged with a serious misdemeanour if they fail to allow the elected or appointed employee representatives to sit in an organ of the employer or other corresponding body in a company, a cooperative or a public institution (Article 228(1)(31) of the Labour Act).

Chapter 4. Collective Bargaining

§1. Level and Scope of Collective Bargaining

169. Articles 192 through 204 of the Labour Act deal with collective agreements. A collective agreement is an agreement concluded as a result of collective bargaining between the representatives of the employees (in the Croatian legal system, these are exclusively representative trade unions or higher-level trade union associations) and of the employer(s) in writing. When a collective agreement is concluded by a single employer and the trade unions, legal literature terms it a company collective agreement; when it is concluded by an employers' association and a trade union association, it is called an association-level collective agreement. The legal provision about the parties to the collective agreement indicates that in Croatia, there are company collective agreements (binding on a single employer), sectoral (branch) collective agreements (concluded on the level of a sector or a branch of industry, binding on all the employers in the sector/all the employers in the branch of industry) and national collective agreements (concluded at the national level, binding on all the employers). Most of the collective agreements in Croatia have been concluded at the level of single employers, i.e., they are company collective agreements. As for the branch collective agreements, it must be noted that once they are concluded, the interest in the regulation of the rights by further collective agreements does not wane: in addition to the branch collective agreements, there is a series of company agreements in each branch. Many of them have been concluded after the conclusion of the branch collective agreement. This practice renders the role of branch collective agreements somewhat questionable. National collective agreements are few and far between. It is worth mentioning that the collective agreement coverage is significantly higher in the public sector than in the private sector.

170. The basic purpose of collective bargaining and collective agreements is to set the salaries and other working conditions of an employer in a branch of industry or sector. The secondary objectives of collective bargaining and collective agreements are to regulate the relations of the parties to the agreement, to resolve collective disputes, to promote the participation of employees in the decision-making, etc.

171. As regards the legal history of collective bargaining in Croatia, it must be noted that collective agreements first appeared in the late nineteenth century. In the 1930s, there was a widespread practice of collective agreements in Yugoslavia, and this continued until the nationalization of private companies and the socialist era. The advent of workers' self-management made collective agreements redundant because, in this period, the prevailing ideological position was that there were no opposing sides in the employment relationship. Workers' self-management means that employees manage the means of production. In this situation, there is no need for collective bargaining because employees have no one to negotiate with. The democratic changes in 1990 and 1991 created conditions for collective bargaining, and the entry into force of the Labour Act of 1995 on 1 January 1996 created the legal framework for collective agreements.

§2. Parties to a Collective Agreement

172. In Croatia, trade unions have the exclusive right to collective bargaining and agreements, representing the employees. According to Article 25(1) of the Act on Representativeness of Employers' Associations and Trade Unions of 2014 (amended in 2015), parties to a collective agreement may be, on the employer side, one or more employers or their associations, and, on the trade union side, a trade. This refers to the private sector. The specificity regarding the parties of collective agreements in the public sector is that, on the side of the employer, the party is the Government of Croatia. Higher-level employers' associations and higher-level trade union associations can be parties to a collective agreement when a collective agreement would apply to employees employed by employers associated with a higher-level employers' association. In order to be parties to a collective agreement, such higher-level associations must be representative of participation in tripartite bodies at the national level. In both sectors (private and public), the parties have to be representative in accordance with the Act on Representativeness of Employers' Associations and Trade Unions. Obviously, there is no need to determine its representativeness when at the level for which the conclusion of a collective agreement is negotiated, only one trade union operates, but when more than one trade union operate at the level for which the collective agreement is negotiated, all trade unions operating at that level may determine by written agreement which trade unions they consider representative. However, when they do not reach an agreement, the representativeness is determined by the Commission for Determining Representativeness (Article 7 of the Act on Representativeness of Employers' Associations and Trade Unions). The Commission consists of five members and five deputy members who are independent academics, judicial officials or prominent experts appointed by the Minister of Labour for a period of five years. Two members and two deputies are appointed at the proposal of trade unions, and two members and two deputies are appointed at the proposal of employers' associations (Article 15(3) of the Act on Representativeness of Employers' Associations and Trade Unions). The Commission for Representativeness determines representativeness for collective bargaining based on criteria set by the Act. Namely, a representative trade union is a trade union that has at least 20% of the total number of union-organized employees employed at the level at which representativeness is determined (Article 8(1) of the Act on Representativeness of Employers' Associations and Trade Unions). In the period 2012–2020, the Commission for Representativeness determined the representativeness of trade unions in 201 cases. In the same period, there were 277 cases in which the trade unions reached the agreement on representativeness by themselves and 648 cases in which there was no need to determine representativeness because, at the level for which the conclusion of collective agreements was negotiated, only one trade union operated (Source: Ministry of Labour, Pension System, Family and Social Policy 7 December 2020). When there are several representative trade unions operating at the level for which the collective agreement is concluded, the employer or employers' association may negotiate only with a negotiating committee consisting of representatives of those unions (Article 9(1) of the Act on Representativeness of Employers' Associations and Trade Unions). Representativeness of trade unions and their representation in the negotiating committee last during the period of validity of the collective agreement (Article 10(1) of the Act on Representativeness of Employers' Associations and Trade Unions). It is worth mentioning that the collective agreement is valid only if the representative trade unions' signatories have in their membership more than 50% of the members of the total trade union-organized employees in representative unions (Article 26(1) of the Act on Representativeness of Employers' Associations and Trade Unions).

173. The legislator distinguishes the parties to the collective agreements and persons bound by the collective agreement. The phrase 'persons bound by the collective agreement' includes more persons than the parties to the collective agreement. A collective agreement is binding on all persons who have concluded it (parties to the collective agreement) and on all persons who, at the time of the conclusion of such an agreement, were or subsequently have become members of the association which is a party to the collective agreement (Article 194(1) of the Labour Act).

§3. Content and Effect of a Collective Agreement

174. Article 192 of the Labour Act regulates the content of a collective agreement in the following way:

> A collective agreement regulates the rights and obligations of the parties that have concluded this agreement. It may also contain legal rules governing the conclusion, contents and termination of employment contracts, social security issues, and other issues arising from or related to employment. The legal rules contained in the collective agreement are directly applicable and binding on all persons who are subject to the collective agreement, in accordance with this Act. A collective agreement may contain rules related to the composition and methods of work of the bodies authorized for amicable collective labour dispute resolution.

I. Obligatory Part

175. Every collective agreement contains provisions stipulating the rights and obligations of the parties to the collective agreement. This is called the obligatory part of the collective agreement. It is customary to include the provisions on the duration of the collective agreements, amendments and renewals, and the provisions on amicable resolution of collective labour disputes through mediation and arbitration. Sometimes, the agreement contains a provision establishing a joint commission for the interpretation of the relevant collective agreement. The effect of a collective agreement is the so-called peace obligation (no-strike clause). Peace obligation after the conclusion of a collective agreement is not explicitly stipulated by law, but it is implicit unless the parties to the collective agreement do not stipulate otherwise in the collective agreement itself. To ensure legal certainty, the parties to the collective agreement often include the no-strike clause in the content of the collective agreement. This clause requires the parties to refrain from industrial action during the time the collective agreement is in force in the matters regulated in the agreement. Since industrial action is a lever the trade unions use against the employer in the process of collective bargaining whose objective is a collective agreement, peace obligation (no industrial action) is, on the one hand, the price paid by the trade union to ensure the best possible result in the negotiations and, on the other hand, a benefit the employer obtains for the concessions they have made in the process of concluding the collective agreement.

II. Normative Part

176. The normative part of the collective agreement is directly applicable and binding on all persons who are subject to the collective agreement (Article 192(2) of the Labour Act). The principle *in favorem laboratoris* does allow the parties to an employment contract to stipulate more favourable terms for the employees, going beyond the rights guaranteed in the collective agreement (stems from Article 9(3) of the Labour Act). Normative provisions of the collective agreement have a direct effect: they are considered part of the employment contracts for all the employees working for the employer who is bound by the collective agreement, regardless of whether they are members of the trade union that signed the collective agreement (inside employees) or not (outside employees). This stems from the legal prohibition of discrimination based on trade union membership. There have been no cases in the domestic case law of unequal treatment of the non-trade union members by the employers in the application of the collective agreement; jurisprudence has indirectly reaffirmed the application of the collective agreement to all the employers working for an employer bound by the collective agreement, as in the disputes related to the rights from collective agreements, the courts do not ask the employees to prove their trade union membership.

There is no explicit legal provision prohibiting the inclusion in a collective agreement of a clause envisaging that an employer must apply the normative provisions of the collective agreement exclusively to the employees who belong to the trade union that has negotiated the benefits (the so-called *differential treatment clause*). However, such clauses are in contravention of Article 14(1) of the Constitution of the Republic of Croatia, which prohibits discrimination on any ground in an open-ended clause.

Of course, the trade unions are fighting against this interpretation because they do not want the non-members to enjoy the benefits they have managed to negotiate for their members. Notable in this context is the repealed provision of the Labour Act mentioned above, which envisaged a negotiation fee. This provision stood in the Labour Act for less than two years (from 2003 to 2005). According to the repealed provision, the collective agreement could compel non-trade union members to pay a fee for the benefits negotiated in the collective agreement for the duration of this agreement. If a collective agreement stipulated a negotiation fee, the agreement entered into force if the employees in the area covered by the collective agreement voted for it in a referendum. The referendum was deemed valid if at least one-third of the employees in the area covered by the collective agreement participated and if more than half of the employees who went to the ballots voted in favour. Thus, if a collective agreement contained a negotiating fee clause, its entry into force depended on the employees' referendum; it was possible for the referendum to fail if not enough employees went to the ballots (at least a third of all the employees in the area covered by the collective agreement) or if less than half of the employees who went to the ballots voted for it. In this case, the collective agreement did not enter into force. However, the reasoning was that the very low quota for the employees who have to go to the ballots and the simple majority requirement would not hinder the entry into force of collective agreements. Furthermore, the provision was that the negotiation fee could not exceed 65% of the trade union membership fee paid by the members to the trade union which signed the collective agreement; if the collective agreement was signed by several trade unions, the negotiation fee could not exceed 65% of the average membership fee in the trade unions that signed the collective agreement. It could also not exceed 1% of the employees' net salary. As stated above, the Constitutional Court repealed the provision of the negotiation fee as unconstitutional, invoking the freedom of association in the reasoning (Articles 43 and 59 of the Constitution), which includes the freedom not to be a member of an association. According to the position taken by the Constitutional Court, the imposition on the non-members of the trade unions of an obligation to finance the trade unions' activities is contrary to the freedom of association guaranteed by the Constitution (Decision of the Constitutional Court of the Republic of Croatia No. U-I-2766/2003 of 2005).

§4. Formal Requirements, Duration

177. In Croatia, a collective agreement is a formal contract. In order for it to be valid, a collective agreement must be concluded in writing (Article 195 of the Labour Act). Every collective agreement and every change (amendment, supplement or termination) to a collective agreement must be submitted, depending on the area of its application, to the ministry or to the competent administrative body. A collective agreement or any changes to a collective agreement applicable in the territory of entire Croatia or in the territory of two or more counties must be submitted to the ministry in charge of labour affairs. All the other collective agreements and changes to the collective agreements must be submitted to the competent administrative body (Article 201(1–2) of the Labour Act). Furthermore, the employers' association or a higher-level employers' association must submit to the competent body a list of employers bound by the collective agreement concluded by the employers' association or the higher-level association, as well as all changes to the association's membership that may have occurred during the period of the collective agreement's validity (Article 201(4) of the Labour Act). If an employer fails to submit the collective agreement or any changes thereto to the relevant body and if they fail to publish it in the manner stipulated by the law (*see* paragraph 179 for more details), misdemeanour proceedings will be instituted against them. This omission is considered a grave misdemeanour and is punishable by a fine of between EUR 660 and EUR 2.650.

178. Because of its normative effect, a collective agreement must be published (Article 202(1) of the Labour Act). The party representing the employers is under an obligation to publish the collective agreement. The employer's failure to publish the collective agreement they are bound by does not affect the obligations arising from the collective agreement (Article 202(3) of the Labour Act). This means in effect that the publication of a collective agreement is not a prerequisite for its implementation; collective agreements enter into force and are implemented in the manner stipulated in the agreement itself, regardless of their publication. This has obviated the very real danger that employers may obstruct the implementation of the collective agreement. The situation is similar to the submission of collective agreements because the relevant bodies that receive the agreements are not authorized to control the contents and validity of the collective agreements. They merely have to make a record of the collective agreements. A collective agreement or any changes thereto must be published within thirty days of its conclusion or of the changes thereto (Article 5 of the Ordinance on the Manner of Publication of Collective Agreements of 2014). According to Article 3 of the Ordinance on the Manner of Publication of Collective Agreements of 2014, collective agreements or any changes thereto which apply in the entire territory of Croatia or in the territory of two or more counties must be published in the Official Gazette. The collective agreements or any changes thereto that apply in a single county must be published in the official gazette of the county. A collective agreement or any changes thereto which bind only one employer must be published by the employer in the same way as the employment regulations; this means that the employer must post the collective agreement in the workplace. In other words, the employer must publish the collective agreement in such a way that it is accessible to all the employees and that it is visibly posted on the premises where employees regularly spend their time during working hours. If this is not possible for a justified reason, the employer must, as soon as the collective agreement is signed, notify the employees of its signing by posting a written notice in a visible place on the premises or through a person in charge of a group of employees, and designate the person or persons who may present the collective agreement to the employees during working hours for their perusal; the collective agreement can also be published on a computer network (intranet).

179. According to Article 198 of the Labour Act, a collective agreement may be concluded for a definite or an indefinite period. When it is concluded for a definite period, this period may not exceed five years. A collective agreement concluded for an indefinite period may be terminated. A collective agreement concluded for a definite period may be terminated only if it contains a termination clause. Both types of collective agreements must contain clauses stating the possible reasons for termination and notice periods. If a collective agreement may be terminated, but parties to a collective agreement have failed to regulate the notice period, according to Article 200(5) of the Labour Act, the notice period is three months.

180. The after-effect of the collective agreement is regulated by Article 199 of the Labour Act.

After the expiration of the period for which this collective agreement was concluded, the legal rules contained therein relating to the conclusion, the contents and termination of employment contracts shall continue to be applicable until a new collective agreement is concluded within a period of three months from the expiration of the term for which the collective agreement was concluded, i.e., three months from the expiration of the notice period as part of the previously concluded employment contracts, but the after-effect cannot exceed a period of three months from the expiry of the period may be agreed upon by a collective agreement. One can conclude that the after-effect of the collective agreement is guaranteed in both cases: when the collective agreement has been terminated by one of the contracting parties and in the case when the term of the fixed-term collective agreement expires. The purpose of the after-effect of the collective agreements is to fill the lacunae in the regulations concerning working conditions (salary, work schedule, length of annual leave, notice period, right to severance pay) arising in the period preceding a new collective agreement and following the expiry of the previous collective agreement. Such lacunae occur whenever a collective agreement ceases to exist, not only after the expiration of the period for which this collective agreement was concluded.

Until 28 July 2012, it was regulated by Article 262 of the repealed Labour Act in the following way:

> Unless otherwise specified by the collective agreement in question, following the expiration of the period for which this collective agreement was concluded, the legal rules contained therein relating to the conclusion, the contents and termination of employment contracts shall continue to be applicable until a new collective agreement is concluded, as part of the previously concluded employment contracts.

Thus, according to this repealed provision, if the parties to the collective agreement did not rule out or otherwise regulate the after-effect of the collective agreement, then the normative part of the collective agreement (provisions regulating the conclusion, contents and termination of individual employment) would continue to apply until a new collective agreement is concluded, as part of the previously concluded employment contracts. It must be noted that the parties to the agreement seldom envisage the exclusion or temporal restriction of the after-effect of the collective agreement in practice. This is because the trade unions consider this to be a major concession to the employer, and they seek in return from the employer the kind of concessions the employer is unwilling to make. In May 2010, the Government of Croatia mooted an amendment to this provision: the after-effect was to be restricted to a maximum of six months after the expiry of the collective agreement. In the statement of reasons, the Government noted that it was unable to comply with its obligations arising from the after-effect of the collective agreements in the civil and public services; these collective agreements had been concluded in a more favourable economic situation. Moreover, the Government was motivated to change the after-effect rule by the fact that the current legal framework (which stipulates that the normative part of the collective agreement is applicable until a new collective agreement is concluded) resulted in a lack of interest in the conclusion of new collective agreements on the part of the trade unions. This proposal engendered a furious reaction among the trade unions, which organized a petition for a referendum to amend the Labour Act and were able to collect a lot of signatures (717,149) in a very short time; they wanted to prevent the amendment of the provision on the after-effect of the collective agreements. All this prompted the Government of Croatia to withdraw the proposal from the legislative procedure.

The Constitutional Court issued its ruling (U-VIIR-4696/2010 of 20 October 2010) stating that this action vacated the conditions for a referendum and setting a time period of a year in which the Government must not submit the same proposal to the legislative procedure. When this period has expired, the legislator has decided to limit the duration of the after-effect of the collective agreement.

It is worth mentioning that the language of the current provision indicates that the after-effect applies only to the employees who had valid employment contracts at the time when the collective agreement was in force, not to those employees who concluded their employment contracts during the after-effect. This regulation creates the problem of unequal employment or working conditions for various employees (possibly even employees who perform equal work or work of equal value) working for the same employer. The same problem arises when a plant or a company is transferred to a new employer, i.e., when employment contracts are transferred to a new employer. In this case, in line with Article 137(12) of the Labour Act, the collective agreement that applied to them before the change of employers continues to apply until a new collective agreement is concluded, but not longer than a year. The purpose of this provision is to prevent employers from evading the obligations of the collective agreement in situations where there are any changes in the status or when plants or companies are transferred in another way. And yet, this provision loses its purpose when a new employer is bound by a collective agreement that envisages more favourable working conditions for the employees than the collective agreement in the after-effect period. As this is a peremptory norm (*ius cogens*), in that case, the new employer must apply to the employees of the transferred plant/company one collective agreement and to the remaining employees another collective agreement (the one binding the employer from the previous period). Because of the application of two different collective agreements, as a result of the compliance with the conditions defined by the law, there might be anti-discrimination lawsuits because of the unequal pay for men and women for equal work or work of equal value. At any rate, there remains the problem of different working conditions for different employees working for the same employer.

181. Although the Labour Act mentions only the expiry of the time period for which the collective agreement was concluded (*see* paragraph 181 on the after-effect of collective agreements) and termination as two ways in which a collective agreement may cease to be in force, given its contractual nature, it should be surmised that a collective agreement may cease to exist by an agreement of the parties thereto and by the conclusion of a new collective agreement which regulates the same issues in a different manner. Since the collective agreement is a contract in light of the mechanism of its formation, according to Article 8(4) of the Labour Act, the conclusion, validity, termination or any other issues pertaining to the collective agreements that are not regulated by the Labour Act or other laws, shall be governed by the obligations law, in line with the nature of this contract. Thus, as regards the cessation of the collective agreement, the following provisions of the Obligations Act must be taken into account: Article 322 (invalidity of a contract), Article 331 (cancellation of a contract), Article 360 (termination of a contract for failure to fulfil contractual obligation) and Article 369 (termination of a contract because of changes in circumstances).

182. Both collective agreements concluded for an indefinite period and those concluded for a definite period may be terminated only if they contain a termination clause (Article 200(1)(2) of the Labour Act). Most of the collective agreements in Croatia are concluded for a definite period; as a rule, they envisage the possibility of a termination, the duration of the notice period, and, rather more seldom, causes for termination (for instance, these cause may include substantial changes in the economic situation and violations of the obligations arising from the agreement). This has made the collective agreements legal sources offering a low level of certainty to the parties. A collective agreement concluded for an indefinite period and a collective agreement concluded for a definite period must contain clauses on the reasons for the termination and notice periods. If a collective agreement may be cancelled, but parties to a collective agreement have failed to regulate the notice period, according to Article 200(5) of the Labour Act, the termination period is three months. A collective agreement must contain the provisions on the amendment and renewal procedures (Article 200(7) of the Labour Act). The Labour Act speaks not only about notice periods but also about causes for termination, which means that the termination of a collective agreement may be predicated on specific causes. In this case, the termination cause stated in the collective agreement must come into being for the collective agreement to be terminated; in other words, it would not be sufficient to merely terminate the agreement by honouring the notice period. *Argumentum a maiori ad minus* and the principle of the freedom of contract make it possible for the parties to the agreement to partially terminate the collective agreement: only some (not all) provisions contained therein may be terminated. According to Article 200(6) of the Labour Act, a notice of termination must be served on all the parties to a collective agreement. In other words, the service of the notice of termination to the other party to the agreement is a prerequisite for the termination to be valid. Furthermore, the notice of the termination of a collective agreement must be submitted, depending on the area of its application, to the Ministry or to the competent administrative body (Article 201(2) of the Labour Act). In most cases, collective agreements cease to be valid because of the expiry of the time period for which they were concluded. Most of the collective agreements in Croatia are concluded for a definite period of time, and they cease to be valid once the time has expired (*see* paragraph 181 on the after-effect of collective agreements). Terminations of collective agreements concluded for a definite time are rare. Freedom of contract makes it possible for the parties to a collective agreement to agree on the provision on the termination of its validity, although termination by mutual consent of the parties to a collective agreement is not explicitly stipulated in the Labour Act. Just as collective agreements must be concluded in writing, the agreement on the termination of a collective agreement should also be made in writing. The Labour Act makes no mention of the possibility of the termination of a collective agreement by the conclusion of a new agreement. This possibility was envisaged in a single specific case in the first version of the Labour Act of 1995. The repealed Article 232 of the Labour Act envisaged the conclusion of a new collective agreement as a way of the termination of the collective agreements concluded before the entry into force of the Labour Act. Although the Labour Act does not stipulate directly that the conclusion of a new collective agreement is a way in which an earlier collective agreement may cease to be valid, it is undoubted that this is indeed a way in which collective agreements may cease to be valid.

§5. Extension of Collective Agreements by Governmental Decree

183. Article 203 of the Labour Act envisages the one exception to the principle of voluntary nature of collective agreements: the extension of the application of a collective agreement to persons who have not taken part in its conclusion and who have not acceded to it subsequently. The general conclusion is that the Croatian collective bargaining system is characterized by the freedom to negotiate as a principle combined with the system of extension by administrative authorities (Minister of Labour). If there is a public interest, the minister in charge of labour may, at the proposal of all parties to a collective agreement, extend the application of the representative collective agreement (concluded with an employers' association or a higher-level employers' association) to employers who are not members of an employers' association or a higher-level employers' association. The minister may decide to extend the application of a collective agreement if an impact assessment reveals there is a clear public interest in the extension of the collective agreement and if it has been determined that the collective agreement has been concluded by the trade unions which have the largest number of members and the employers' associations with the largest number of employees in the area to which the application is to be extended (this is the representativeness of the collective agreement). The minister decides whether there is a public interest in the extension of a collective agreement based on the number and structure of employers to which collective agreement will be extended, based on the data on the number of employees and the level of rights of employees and after consulting with representatives of employers to which the collective agreement will be extended. The minister must specify the scope of the application of the collective agreement whose extension is under consideration. This decision must be published in the Official Gazette. The Labour Minister is obliged to repeal the decision on the extension of the application of the collective agreement when the collective agreement has been amended or renewed, and the parties to the collective agreement have not to make a proposal for the extension of amended or renewed collective agreement within thirty days from the date of delivery of the amendment or renewal. The expiry of the duration of the collective agreement whose application has been extended inevitably results in the termination of the extended application because there is no original collective agreement and thus no public interest, which had led to the extension of the application of the collective agreement. This is explicitly stated in Article 203(5) of the Labour Act. For instance, the application of the collective agreement for the hospitality sector has been extended recently (Official Gazette No. 49/2024).

The following elements were stated as matters of public interest in the decisions to extend the application of the existing collective agreements so far: equalizing the minimum working and employment conditions in a branch of industry, providing greater social stability within a branch of industry (as a result of an improvement in the financial and social status of a greater segment of employees within the branch), eliminating the disruptions to the competition on the market caused by cheap labour by the employers not bound by the collective agreement and fighting illegal work and grey economy.

§6. Enforcement of the Collective Agreement

184. A party to a collective agreement may bring an action before the competent court to seek judicial protection of the rights arising from such an agreement (Article 204 of the Labour Act). This provision guarantees judicial protection in cases of collective disputes of rights (disputes involving the application of the obligatory provisions of the collective agreements such as, , the disputes on the termination of the collective agreement or the implementation of the rules on amicable resolution of collective disputes stipulated in the collective agreement). The courts do not have jurisdiction to resolve interest disputes or to define tasks that must not be discontinued during a strike or lock-out. The judicial jurisdiction in deciding on the prohibition of a strike or lock-out is discussed in paragraph 192. The parties to a dispute may agree to stipulate that any disputes be resolved not in a court of law but by a court of arbitration. According to Article 212(1) of the Labour Act, if a dispute concerns the application of a collective agreement, the arbitration body must base its decision on the collective agreement. The arbitration body can base its decision on equitable grounds (*ex aequo et bono*) only if a dispute concerns the conclusion, amendment or renewal of a collective agreement.

185. Since the normative provisions of a collective agreement are incorporated into all employment contracts as their integral part, if the employer violates the employment contract, the employees have *locus standi* before a competent court. In Zagreb, the jurisdiction lies with the Municipal Labour Court, and in the rest of Croatia, the municipal courts – courts of general jurisdiction – deal with such cases.

Chapter 5. Industrial Conflict

§1. Strikes

186. The Constitution guarantees the right to strike in its Article 60(1). This right is regulated in greater detail in the provisions of the Labour Act. Strikes are a way in which collective labour disputes can be resolved through conflict; they are an exclusive right of the trade unions and their associations. Only they can call for and organize a strike action. Article 205(2) of the Labour Act prescribes that in the event of a dispute over the conclusion, amendment or renewal of a collective agreement, only representative trade unions (trade unions that are declared representative in line with the Act on Representativeness of Employers' Associations and Trade Unions; *see* paragraph 173) which have negotiated a collective agreement are entitled to call for a strike. There have been cases when the work stoppage by discontented employees was not initiated by a trade union. A strike that has not been organized by a trade union is illegal and banned (VSRH, Gž-16/00 of 10 May 2000 and Revr-482/05 of 25 October 2005, Gž-16/99 of 15 June 1999 and Varaždin County Court, Gž-321/02 of 18 March 2003). The sanctions for participation in an unauthorized strike are (extraordinary) dismissal and the liability for the damage caused by the strike (for more details, *see* paragraph 192). For a strike to be legal, it must be organized by a trade union. Furthermore, there must be justified reasons for a strike; the strike must be declared in advance and must follow a compulsory mediation procedure (the only exceptions are sympathy or solidarity/secondary strikes). These prerequisites are cumulative. If any one of the prerequisites for the legality of a strike is not met, the strike is illegal (VSRH, P-2/00 of 10 May 2000).

187. According to Article 205(1) of the Labour Act, a strike can be organized in order to protect and promote the economic and social interest of trade union members or because of the failure of the employer to pay salary, part of salary or salary compensation if not paid by the due date. In the initial text of the Labour Act of 1995, the right to strike because the employees have not received their salary was not envisaged. This right was introduced in the amendments of 2001 because of the habit developed by Croatian employers not to pay their employees. The initial idea was to allow strikes only where there were disputes involving collective interests, not in collective legal disputes (where recourse was to be sought in court). Sympathy strikes were legalized in 2003. A sympathy strike may begin two days after the date of the commencement of the strike the sympathy strike supports. Sympathy strikes may be staged even if the mediation procedure has not been followed through (Article 205(5) of the Labour Act).

188. In order for the strike to be allowed, it must be declared in advance. A strike must be declared in advance to the employer or to the employers' association against which it is directed; a sympathy strike must be declared in advance to the employer on whose premises it is organized (Article 205(3) of the Labour Act). A letter declaring the strike must state the reasons for the strike, the place, date, time of its commencement and the manner of its undertaking (Article 205(6) of the Labour Act).

As noted above, the procedural prerequisite for a strike to be allowed is the mediation process. The disputing parties may agree to a different amicable resolution procedure. The mediation procedure is conducted by a mediator, who is elected by the disputing parties from a list put together by the Economic and Social Council or by mutual agreement. The rule is for the mediation to be conducted by a single mediator, but the parties may agree on more (Article 5 of the Ordinance on the Selection of Mediators and the Mediation Process in Collective Labour Disputes of 2015, amended in 2020). This Ordinance envisages the mechanism for the selection of mediators when the parties cannot agree on it. In that case, the decision to appoint the mediator for the case in question is made by the chairperson of the Economic and Social Council or the minister if the Economic and Social Council has not been established or ceased to function. The Labour Act stipulates that the mediation process must be completed within five days of the date when the notice of the dispute was submitted to the Economic and Social Council, the ministry or a competent administrative body, unless the parties have agreed differently, which means that the mediation may take more or less time (VSRH, Gž-1/02 of 16 January 2002). The mediator must strive for the disputing parties to achieve an agreement in the course of the mediation process. The mediator submits a written proposal of the solutions for the contentious issues and sets deadlines for the parties for their acceptance or refusal. The mediator drafts an agreement if the disputing parties have accepted the proposal or if they have reached an agreement about the contentious issues. The conclusion of an agreement on the contentious issues completes the mediation process, and the mediator must notify the Economic and Social Council (or the Ministry of Labour when the Economic and Social Council has not been established or ceased to function) accordingly. If the mediation process has failed, the mediator again notifies the Council. A written finding that the mediation process has failed is important for the trade unions because the completion of the mediation process is a prerequisite for strike action. An agreement reached in a dispute about the conclusion, amendment or renewal of a collective agreement has the same legal force and effects as a collective agreement (Article 209(2) of the Labour Act). If the mediation process failed, the employees go on strike or engage in some other form of industrial action; there are cases, however, when the parties prefer to present the dispute to the court of arbitration. Unlike the mediation process in which the parties are free to accept or refuse the proposal made by the mediator, the decision of the court of arbitration is binding: the issue on which the court of arbitration has ruled may not be a cause for a strike or other industrial action. This is why the trade unions rarely agree to allow arbitration in collective interest disputes. However, in practice, there have been cases of forced arbitration in the determination of jobs that must not be stopped during a strike. The Labour Act thus contains an exception to the rule that arbitration in dispute resolution is voluntary. When a trade union and an employer fail to reach an agreement on jobs (essential assignments and production maintenance assignments) that must not be stopped during a strike, the decision is taken by the court of arbitration. In that case, the dispute may be brought before the court of arbitration by a single party, and the proceedings may be conducted even if the other party does not take part in the appointment of the president of the arbitration chamber and in the arbitration itself. According to Article 214 of the Labour Act, at the proposal of the employer, the trade union and the employer prepare and adopt, by mutual agreement, the rules that apply to production maintenance assignments and essential assignments, which must not be stopped during a strike or a lock-out. These rules include, in particular, the provisions concerning assignments and the number of employees who must perform these assignments during a strike or a lock-out in order for normal work to resume immediately after the strike ('the production maintenance assignments'), or in order to carry out tasks essential for the prevention of risk to life, personal safety or health of the population ('the essential assignments'). The definition of the assignments must not prevent or substantially restrict the right to strike (by unnecessarily defining them too broadly). If the trade union and the employer do not reach an agreement on these assignments within fifteen days of the day when the employer's proposal was forwarded to the trade union, the employer or the trade union may, within the next fifteen days, request that these assignments be defined by an arbitration body.

The arbitration body consists of a representative of the trade union, a representative of the employer and an independent chairperson who is appointed by mutual agreement between the trade union and the employer. If the trade union and the employer fail to reach an agreement about the appointment of the chairperson of the arbitration board, and if these issues are not otherwise regulated by a collective agreement or an agreement between the parties, the chairperson is appointed by the president of the court which has the jurisdiction to hear cases related to the prohibition of a strike or a lock-out. If one of the parties refuses to participate in an arbitration procedure aimed at defining the assignments which must not be stopped, the procedure can be completed without the participation of this party and a decision on the assignments which must not be stopped during a strike or a lock-out is rendered by the chairperson of the arbitration body. The arbitration body must render a decision on the assignments within fifteen days after the arbitration procedure began. In order to prevent the obstruction of a strike action by an employer, the legislator has set a deadline by which the employer can initiate the proceedings to define the assignments: if the employer proposed that the assignments be defined after the start of the mediation procedure, the procedure to define the assignments may not be initiated until the end of the strike (Article 214(9) of the Labour Act). Legal theory has taken the stand that the refusal during a strike by the employees to perform assignments that must not be stopped constitutes participation in an unauthorized strike. This is a serious violation of the employment obligations, and the employer may dismiss the employee for that cause (the dismissal may be extraordinary). A *lex specialis* thus explicitly notes that the contracts of employment of the healthcare employees terminate in the case when they refuse to perform crucial tasks that must be performed at all times in order to prevent risk to life or health of patients (Article 199(7) of the Health Care Act of 2018, last amended in 2020).

189. The prerequisites for an authorized strike listed above are contained in the Labour Act. This law envisages that collective agreements and trade union rules may list substantive and procedural prerequisites for authorized strikes (it stems from Article 215(1) of the Labour Act). In practice, some collective agreements contain a broader set of causes for an authorized strike, going beyond the causes listed in the law. The Supreme Court has taken the position that a collective agreement may stipulate that a strike is authorized in the case of legal disputes, i.e., when the provisions of the collective agreement have been violated or when the rights arising from employment and related to employment have been violated (VSRH, Gž-5/00 of 13 April 2000). There is a dilemma about the issue of whether the right to strike may be restricted by the provisions of a collective agreement. There have been no cases when the right to strike was restricted by a collective agreement, but the freedom of contract indicates that such restrictions would be permissible.

190. The right to strike cannot exist if the strikers do not have a guarantee they will not suffer any negative consequences of their participation in a legally organized strike. This guarantee is contained in Article 215 of the Labour Act:

> The organization of a strike or participation in a strike organized in compliance with the law, collective agreement and trade union rules do not constitute a violation of an employment contract. An employee must not be placed in a less favourable position than other employees because of his or her involvement in the organization of or participation in a strike organized in compliance with the law, collective agreement and trade union rules. An employee may be dismissed only if he or she organizes or participates in a strike non-compliant with the law, collective agreement or trade union rules, or if in the course of strike he or she commits some other grave violation of an employment contract. An employee must not, by any means, be coerced into participating in a strike.

The only consequence that employees may suffer as a consequence of their participation in a legally organized strike is a reduction in salary and salary supplements. The reduction must be proportionate to the time spent on strike (Article 216 of the Labour Act).

191. The Labour Act contains provisions on the judicial prohibition of an illegal strike and lock-out and the compensation for the damage caused by such actions (Articles 217 and 218) and the provision on the judicial jurisdiction to prohibit a strike or a lock-out (Article 219). An employer or an employers' association may petition the court that has jurisdiction to prohibit the organization of an illegal strike and the strike itself. An employer may claim compensation for the damage suffered as a result of an illegal strike. A trade union may petition the court that has jurisdiction to prohibit an illegal lock-out and claim compensation for the damage suffered by the trade union or the employees as a result of an illegal lock-out.

192. Strike actions in the armed forces, police, public administration and public services are regulated by *leges specialis*: the Police Act, the Service in the Armed Forces Act and the Health Care Act. According to Article 39(1) of the Police Act of 2011 (last amended in 2023), police officers do not have the right to strike in the following cases: state of war or an imminent threat to the independence and territorial integrity of the state, armed rebellion, uprising and other forms of violent threats to the democratic and constitutional order of Croatia or the fundamental human and civil rights and liberties, declared natural disasters or imminent threat of a natural disaster in the territory of two or more counties or in entire Croatia, other disasters and accidents that affect normal life and threaten the safety of people and property. According to Article 39(2) of the Police Act, police officers must exercise police powers even while they are on strike if such actions are required to protect the lives and safety of the people, to arrest and remand in custody persons caught in the course of the perpetration of a criminal offence that is prosecutable ex officio, and to prevent the perpetration and identify the perpetrators of criminal offences prosecutable ex officio. According to Article 15 of the Service in the Armed Forces Act of 2013 (last amended in 2024), active-duty service personnel are not allowed to strike; non-combat personnel employed in the armed forces may, as a rule, go on strike, except during a state of war or an imminent threat to Croatia, or if a strike directly affects the stand-by measures of the civil and military defence, combat readiness of the Armed Forces or if it endangers the vital functions of the Armed Forces. Article 198 of the Health Care Act of 2018 (last amended in 2024) prohibits strikes in healthcare institutions/services of emergency medical assistance.

Strikes in other departments of healthcare institutions may not be staged before the completion of the mediation process, in line with the general regulations on strike actions. As regards the healthcare provided in healthcare institutions, with the exception of emergency medicine, the Ministry of Health and the trade union need to define the crucial activities that must be performed at all times to prevent endangering the life or disability of the patients. If they do not reach an agreement within fifteen days from the day of the submission of the Ministry's proposal on tasks that must be performed at all times, the Ministry or the trade union may initiate arbitration within a further fifteen days.

193. According to the jurisprudence of the VSRH, a work stoppage may be considered a strike even if work has not been stopped fully (VSRH, Gž-16/00 of 10 May 2000): in this case, the employees stopped work, prevented the director and other management personnel from entering the employer's premises and organized work as they saw fit. According to the position taken by the VSRH, this action constitutes a strike rather than another form of industrial action (picketing, boycotting, slow-down strike, etc.). The Supreme Court has also ruled that a meeting of employees that extends over a number of days constitutes an illegal strike (VSRH, Revt-32/05 of 21 September 2005). In this case, the employees were unhappy with the responses they received from the employer, and they held an impermissibly long employees' meeting during which a number of employees did not work at all.

194. No formal decision needs to be taken to stop a strike. For a strike to stop, it is essential for it to have stopped de facto, i.e., that the employees are back at work. The legal effects of the end of a strike are obtained vis-à-vis the employer as of the time the employer is notified about the end of the strike (VSRH, Gž-1/03 of 28 February 2003 and Gž-6/99 of 8 April 1999). Only a situation which clearly and unequivocally indicates that the work has resumed in its entirety, i.e., in the scope and substance that existed before the strike, may be considered an end of a strike (VSRH, Gž-17/98 of 15 September 1998).

195. There are relatively few strikes in Croatia. Most of the collective labour disputes are resolved amicably. The number of strikes, the number of employees participating in strikes and the number of lost working hours clearly show the unwillingness of the trade unions in Croatia to resolve collective labour disputes through strikes.

§2. LOCK-OUTS

196. In some circumstances, the employer may respond to a strike by initiating a lock-out. Only defensive lock-outs are allowed in Croatia, and the employers are further hindered by the provisions restricting the number of employees that may be locked out. According to Article 213 (1 through 3) of the Labour Act, employers may engage in a lock-out only as a response to a strike already in progress. A lock-out must not commence prior to the expiration of eight days from the date of the commencement of a strike, and the number of employees locked out from work must not be higher than one-half of the employees who are on strike. During a lock-out, the fundamental rights and obligations arising from employment are suspended: the employees do not work, and the employers are not obliged to pay their salaries. However, under Article 213(4), the employer must pay mandatory social security contributions for the locked-out employees (20% for pension insurance and 16.5% for unemployment insurance) for the lowest salary base defined by a special regulation. According to the Order on the Bases for the Calculation of the Mandatory Social Security Contributions for 2014 (Official Gazette No. 150/2023), the lowest base is EUR 592.80. Because of these legal constraints, the lock-out has not been used.

197. Article 218 of the Labour Act provides for the judicial prohibition of an illegal lock-out and stipulates the compensation for the damage: a trade union may petition the court that has jurisdiction to prohibit an illegal lock-out and to claim compensation for the damage suffered by this trade union or the employees as a result of an illegal lock-out. This provision does not envisage the right of the employees to be restored to work if there is an illegal lock-out, but the Supreme Court has taken the position that the prohibition of an illegal lock-out is pointless if it does not entail as a sanction the reinstatement of the employees to work from which they have been illegally locked out (VSRH, Gž-11/96 of 13 November 1996).

Selected Bibliography

Legislation

Potočnjak, Ž., & Vukorepa, I., *Zakon o radu i drugi izvori radnog prava*, 2011, Narodne novine, Zagreb.

Cases

Crnić, I., *Otkaz ugovora o radu*, 2013, Organizator, Zagreb.
Crnić, I., *Zakon o radu – Primjena u praksi*, 2012, Organizator, Zagreb.

Journals

Radno pravo (Rosip, Zagreb).
Revija za socijalnu politiku (Pravni fakultet, Zagreb).

Books

Crnić, I. et al. (ed. Potočnjak, Ž.), *Radni odnosi u Republici Hrvatskoj*, 2007, Organizator, Pravni fakultet, Zagreb.
Ravnić, A., *Osnove radnog prava – domaćeg, usporednog i međunarodnog*, 2004, Pravni fakultet, Zagreb.

Websites

The Constitutional Court of the Republic of Croatia: http://www.usud.hr/.
Supreme Court of the Republic of Croatia: http://www.vsrh.hr/.
Official Gazette: http://www.nn.hr/.
Croatian Parliament: http://www.sabor.hr/.
Chair of Labour Law and Social Security Law, Faculty of Law, University of Zagreb: http://www.pravo.unizg.hr/RSP/zakoni.
Croatian Employment Service: http://www.hzz.hr/.

Selected Bibliography

Index

The number here refers to paragraph numbers.

Adoption leave, 48, 77, 124, 130, 131
Annual leave, 28, 47, 68–85, 124, 163, 180
Apprenticeship, 37, 120, 134
Arbitration, 127, 132, 135, 143, 145, 159, 163, 175, 184, 188, 192

Breastfeeding, 47, 72, 82–85, 95–97

Child labour, 17
Collective agreements
  content, 23, 175, 176, 178, 180
  duration, 25, 175–183
  effect, 20, 25, 175, 176, 178, 180–182
  extension, 25, 183
  normative part, 176, 180
  obligatory part, 175
  parties, 23, 25, 51, 169, 170, 172, 173, 175, 176, 179–184
Collective bargaining, 12, 17, 18, 24, 151, 169–185
Collective labour law, 12, 150–197
Contract of employment
  fixed-term, 35, 104
  open-ended, 33, 34, 36, 111
Court decisions, 21, 22, 67

Disabled persons, 19, 39–41, 63
Discrimination, 17, 18, 20, 27, 40, 47, 48, 65–67, 107, 146, 147, 151, 176, 180
Dismissal
  collective, 37, 107, 108, 121, 134, 138, 163, 186, 188
  extraordinary, 111–116, 118, 119, 121, 122, 125, 126, 139, 147, 186, 188
  ordinary, 37, 111, 116, 117, 119–121, 125, 134
Dispute settlement
  in collective labour law, 11
  in individual labour law, 12
Duties of the employee, 50–54
Duties of the employer, 55–67

Employee, 10–12, 14, 20, 23, 26, 27, 29–36, 38–60, 63, 64, 67–75, 77–82, 85–89, 91, 92, 94, 95, 97–112, 114–123, 125–127, 130–133, 135–141, 144–147, 150–152, 155–157, 161–172, 176, 178, 180, 183, 185–188, 190, 191, 193–197
Employee inventions, 139–141
Employee liability, 98–103
Employee participation, 12, 20, 161–168
Employee representation on the supervisory board, 166–168
Employers' associations, 12, 15, 20, 24, 144, 151–160, 169, 172, 177, 183, 186, 188, 191
Employment Office, 42
Equal pay, 62, 86, 92, 93
Equal treatment, 18, 47, 65–67

Foreign employees, 42–45
Freedom of association, 14, 17, 23, 150, 151, 176
Freedom of contract, 108, 182, 189
Full-time employment, 35, 69

Health and safety, 19, 20, 47, 52, 98, 119, 163
Health insurance, 13, 41, 84, 94, 96

Individual employment contract, 33–36
Individual labour law, 11
Industrial actions
  lock-out, 196–197
  strike, 163
Industrial peace, 175

Index

Insolvency, 20, 120, 130
International sources, 17

Juveniles, 38

Lock-out, 142, 143, 184, 188, 191, 196, 197

Managerial employees, 30
Maternity, 13, 20, 48, 49, 72, 77, 82–85, 94–97, 114, 124, 130, 131
Meeting of employees, 193
Minimum wage, 14, 20, 40, 56, 91

Night work, 58, 68, 72, 73, 86, 88, 163
No-strike clause, 175

Occupational disease, 40, 98, 118, 125, 127, 132, 133
Overtime, 47, 58, 68, 70, 71, 86, 88, 163

Parenthood, 48, 114, 130, 131
Part-time employment, 35, 69
Pregnancy, 48, 72, 94–97, 124, 130, 131
Protection against dismissals, 127
Public holidays, 20, 68–85

Remuneration, 17, 32, 55–62, 77, 80, 86–97, 142
Rest period, 11, 20, 30, 47, 75, 78, 79
Retirement, 13, 23, 66, 104, 107
Right to work, 18–20, 94, 124

Self-employed, 10, 40, 42, 85, 96, 97
Sexual harassment, 65, 67, 145, 146, 163
Shift work, 72, 73
Short-time work (reduced working time), 70, 180
Sickness, 94
Social insurance law, 13
Social security law, 13
Sources of labour law, 16–29
Strike
  legal effects, 194
  solidarity strike, 186
Subordination, 30, 32
Sunday work, 58, 74–76, 86, 88
Supervisory Board, 12, 125, 127, 162, 163, 165–168

Temporary work, 36, 94, 103
Termination of contract, 11, 20, 22, 25, 48, 106–139, 155, 174, 180
Termination by mutual consent, 108, 182
Trade unions, 12, 15, 19, 20, 23, 24, 27, 38, 55, 57, 65, 80, 87, 129, 136, 144, 150–160, 162, 163, 169, 172, 175, 176, 180, 183, 186–192, 195, 197

Unemployment insurance, 13, 196
Unemployment rate, 9

Vocational training, 80

Women, 2, 9, 17, 18, 47, 48, 62, 63, 65, 66, 84, 86, 92, 130, 180
Works agreement, 11, 26, 28, 87
Working time, 11, 20, 30, 35, 46, 47, 68–85, 147
Works council, 12, 20, 26, 27, 29, 30, 38, 40, 67, 69, 70, 72, 78, 80, 87, 97, 109, 115, 125–129, 132, 135–138, 146, 156, 161–167

Youth employment, 18, 19

www.ingramcontent.com/pod-product-compliance
Lightning Source LLC
Chambersburg PA
CBHW071352230926
51846CB00002B/518
* 9 7 8 9 4 0 3 5 2 7 8 9 5 *